MONKS, PRIESTS AND PEASANTS

MONOGRAPHS
IN SOCIAL ANTHROPOLOGY AND THEORETICAL STUDIES
IN HONOUR OF NELS ANDERSON

General Editor: K. Ishwaran

Publication 1

MONKS, PRIESTS AND PEASANTS

A STUDY OF BUDDHISM AND SOCIAL STRUCTURE IN CENTRAL CEYLON

BY

HANS-DIETER EVERS

With 27 tables, 10 figures and 8 plates

LEIDEN
E. J. BRILL
1972

PRINTED IN THE NETHERLANDS

CONTENTS

LIST OF TABLES

LIST OF FIGURES

LIST OF PLATES

Introduction

THREE great religious traditions have shaped the destiny of Greater India: Hinduism, Buddhism and Islam. As religious systems they are distinct enough in their canonical scriptures, their symbols and their ways to salvation, and generations of religious specialists have tried to maintain the distinctions. But centuries of peaceful coexistence as well as bitter conflict have at times moved the religious systems closer together or further away from each other in a constantly changing pattern of dominance, equality, fusion and separation. The resulting social and cultural complexity of South and Southeast Asia is unparallelled in Post-Roman Europe, and it may be our own cultural experience and socialization which compels us to think in terms of *one* dominant religion, in terms of reformation or variation instead of competition between completely different religions. This same European world view may also seduce us into accepting a simple classification of Asian societies into Muslim, Buddhist or Hindu. As most Southeast Asian societies and several nations have at present a dominant religion such a classification is perhaps superficially correct, but if we want to understand the social and political structures and dynamics much more detailed and complex categories are necessary.

The culture and social structure of any society is, indeed, extremely complex. No single index, no sophisticated factor analysis has so far been able to analyse the social structure of a whole society and predict its development. Nor is there, I believe, one single correct description of a society and its culture. Depending on the point of view adapted, the level of analysis chosen, and the concepts used, quite different but nevertheless "correct" pictures are bound to emerge. Only by matching the complexity of a social structure and culture with an appropriate number of studies from different angles will it be possible to come to an adequate understanding and analysis. It is perhaps significant that only a few postwar studies are concerned with the religious complexity of Southeast Asian societies. With the exception of Geertz who chose as the locus of his fieldwork and the basis for his generalizations a fairly large and complex social unit, a middle-sized town, anthropologists have usually done village studies and have therefore missed out on some of the more centralized elements of the socio-religious complexity. A village in Ceylon, Thailand or Burma might include a few religious specialists of one or two of the religious systems, e.g. Buddhist monks and village exorcists, but hardly such important institutions as a temple for gods or demons, large monasteries and a royal court. Yet, what would express the basic worldview, the design for societal structure and the moral texture of a society better than these central institutions. Royal palaces and large temples are indeed complex sacred symbols which "function to synthesize a people's ethos—the tone, character, and quality of their life, its moral and aesthetic style and mood—and their world-view—the picture they have of the way things in sheer actuality are, their most comprehensive ideas of order." (Geertz 1966: 3).

In the following study I shall try to analyse such a central institution, a Buddhist temple in Central Ceylon. Whereas most studies by social anthropologists have, as it were, adopted a village point of view for their analysis of Theravada Buddhism I shall look at the religion and social structure of Central Ceylon from the lofty heights of the "Great Royal Temple of Lankatilaka", the former state temple of the Gampola empire. As this will be the first empirical study of a temple and monastery in a Theravada Buddhist country, a good deal of detailed descriptive material will have to be presented. But our effort to understand the basic pattern underlying the complex organization of the temple itself will from time to time be interrupted to look at the socio-religious structure of Southern Buddhism in general, thus adopting a specific point of view for the analysis of a complex social structure and religion.

This book is written for the specialist, either the sociologist and anthropologist of religion or the student of Buddhism and its cultural history in Ceylon and Southeast Asia. I have therefore tried to be as precise as possible. I have refrained from repeating general facts already discussed in other studies and therefore well known to the experienced scholar. As I have been frustrated over and over again myself by reading the same old descriptions of Buddhism I have tried to spare my readers the same experience. Descriptions in this study are nevertheless very detailed, but appear, I believe, for the first time in print. Often I have tried to write a historical document, which will be of use to later students of social and religious change. My gurus in this endeavour have been the 19th century scholars and civil servants who spent year after year studying and describing their host cultures in meticulous detail, rather than the traveling modern social scientist who is tempted to view underdeveloped countries from his airconditioned hotel room or through the survey data collected by his labourious native research assistants. All these detailed descriptions and analyses have, however, not kept me from pointing out their wider significance. The analysis of the royal temple of Lankatilaka thus becomes the analysis of the social structure and basic cultural pattern of Theravada Buddhism.

The present study could not have been written in its concise form without the extensive work, partly still unpublished, of a number of scholars in various disciplines. The work of Ames, Obeyesekere and Yalman has it made possible to exclude discussions on that part of Sinhalese religion often called "magical animism", Bechert's comprehensive study on Buddhism and politics in Ceylon has rendered an originally planned part of this book on the organization of the Buddhist Sangha and its monasteries superfluous, and Gombrich's doctoral thesis on the interpretation of canonical Buddhist concepts by villagers and village monks has reduced my obligation to say more about the Sinhalese Buddhist value system. I am, however, obliged to thank these scholars for their comments on parts of this study and for extensive correspondence and discussions which have helped to clarify a number of issues.

The idea of studying a "traditional" organization and traditional elite was first conccived during an earlier study on the emergence of a class of industrial entrepreneurs in Ceylon. During this 16 months stay in Ceylon 1958–59 and 1961 I collected some preliminary information which I could follow up by library work in the Public Record Office and the British Museum Library in London. Fieldwork was done for 9 months in 1964–65 and during two short visits in 1968 and 1970. Most of this time I lived in one of the temple villages in Central Ceylon. During these prolonged studies a great debt to a number of organizations has accumulated. I am grateful for the support received from Monash University, Melbourne, the American Council of Learned Societies, the Social Science Research Council and the Yale University Concilium on International and Area Studies. A Yale University Senior Faculty Fellowship enabled me to put the final touch to this manuscript in January–February 1970.

I would also like to record my thanks to the staff of the Library, University of Ceylon, Peradeniya, especially to Mr. Somadasa, Librarian; Mr. H. A. I. Goonetileke, Deputy Librarian; and Mr. C. F. Fonseka. Mr. M. Doraswamy typed the manuscript and Mr. Kristian, Department of Geography, University of Ceylon, prepared some of the maps and figures. My most sincere thanks are, however, due to the "monks, priests, and peasants" in Central Ceylon who have patiently answered questions and often extended their hospitality.

Peradeniya, Ceylon H.–D.E.
February 1970

A NOTE ON THE TRANSCRIPTION OF SINHALESE

Sinhalese terms are usually given in their singular form. They have been transcribed according to the system used by Wilhelm Geiger, *A Grammar of the Sinhalese Language*, Colombo: Royal Asiatic Society, 1931. Place names and personal names are usually written in their anglicized forms. Often reoccurring Sinhalese terms are printed without diacritical marks. The correct spelling is found in the glossary or in brackets printed in *italics*. For technical reasons the long *ä* could not be distinguished in print from the short *ä*. Both appear, therefore, as the same character. All Sinhalese terms have been checked in standard dictionaries. In cases of doubt the spelling of Carter's Sinhalese-English Dictionary has been used. A number of terms used by Sinhalese informants could not be found in Carter. Some effort has then been made to trace these terms in other works, e.g. in Epigraphia Zeylanica, Ralph Pieris 1956 or Heinz Bechert 1966 (See Glossary). The spelling as used by village and temple informants has usually been adopted in cases of doubt.

CHAPTER ONE

Modern Theravada Buddhism: The Social Organization of Sinhalese Religion in Central Ceylon

1. Sinhalese religion in action: the Äsala Perahära in Kandy

EVERY year in July or August a great festival takes place in the city of Kandy, the former capital of the last Sinhalese kingdom. Now a tourist attraction because of its oriental splendour and pageantry, it used to be the most important state ritual in the days of the Sinhalese kings. "The presence of the king, the adigars, the chiefs of the great departments of the central government like the Mahalekam, Kodituwakku and Kuruve, the provincial leaders like Dissaves, Korales, Atukorales and vidanes seemed to sum up in the Perahara the politico-administrative structure of the community." (Seneviratne 1963: 177).

But even today the Äsala Perahära has not lost its social significance. It still reflects the social and religious system of the Sinhalese, though it fulfills only insufficiently the classic integrating function of ritual and has become a focus of social conflict rather than integration.

The festival lasts for three weeks during which several prescribed rituals take place. (Seneviratne 1963, Aluwihare 1964, Raghavan 1962: 120–126, Millawa 1817). The most conspicuous events are, however, the processions moving through the streets of Kandy. A typical procession *(perahära)* would consist of the following parts and participants:

1. The *Māḷigāva Perahära* (procession of the Temple of the Buddha's Tooth Relic)
    (a) Whip crackers and flagbearers
    (b) The *Peramunerāḷa* (temple official) riding on an elephant and holding the register of temple lands *(lēkam miṭiya)*
    (c) Musicians, drummers and dancers from various villages who hold temple land for their participation in the procession
    (d) The *Gajanāyaka Nilamē* (the chief of the elephant stables)
    (e) Musicians, drummers and dancers (see c), elephants
    (f) The *Kāriyakōrāla* (chief supervisor of temple services, *rājakāriya*) with other temple officials, drummers and dancers
    (g) The Maligava tusker carrying the casket of the sacred tooth relic

(h) The *Diyavaḍana Nilamē* (the chief temple official and trustee of the *Daḷadā Māḷigāva*) with other temple officials, musicians, drummers and dancers.

2. The *Nātha Dēvāle Perahära* (procession of the temple of God Natha in Kandy) includes musicians, drummers and dancers, mostly temple tenants; the priests of the temple *(kapurāḷa)* in front of an elephant, who carries the weapons of the God *(ranāyudha)* in a howdah *(ranhiligē)* on his back; the chief temple official and trustee *(basnāyaka nilamē)* together with minor temple officials and the basnayakas of other Natha devales, located elsewhere in Central Ceylon, namely the devales of Dodanwela, Wegiriya and Pasgama. They are also accompanied by their priests, temple officials, and temple tenants.
3. The *Mahā Visnu Devāle Perahära* (procession of the temple of God Vishnu in Kandy) resembles the *Nātha Dēvāle Perahära*. The *Basnāyaka Nilamē* is, however, accompanied by representatives of the Lankatilaka, Gadaladeniya, Alavatugoda and Hanguranketa devales.
4. The *Kataragama Dēvāle Perahära* (procession of the temple of God Kataragama in Kandy) is joined by officials and tenants from Embekke and Ganagoda devales.
5. The *Pattini Dēvāla Perahära* (procession of the temple of the Goddess Pattini in Kandy) is similar to the other *dēvāla perahäras*.

The socio-religious structure enacted in these processions consists of three interrelated systems. These are represented during the festival by the *Māḷigāva perahära*, the *dēvāle perahäras* and the presence of the Kandyan nobility. The *Daḷadā Māḷigāva* ("Tooth Relic Palace") is Ceylon's most important center of Buddhist worship. The ritual inside the *Māḷigāva* is conducted by bhikkhus, Buddhist monks, in front of images of the Buddha and a casket with his tooth relic and relics of his disciple Sivali. The ritual language employed is Pali the canonical language of Theravada Buddhism. The ritual in the devales, however, is conducted in Sinhalese or Sanskrit, by kapuralas, married priests, in front of images of the respective gods. The lay organization and administration is also kept apart but is nevertheless strikingly similar in many aspects. Both the Maligava and the devales are administered by chief temple officials and their deputies, the services during the festival from providing supplies and decorations to participation in the processions are performed by temple tenants who hold temple lands (*vihāragam* and *dēvālagam*) in lieu of their *rājakāriya* (lit. "king's work," in this case temple service). The various services cannot, however, be provided by just anyone for each duty is connected with a particular caste. The perahäras thus reflect the social stratification of Sinhalese society.

The two systems which comprise the *Daḷadā Māḷigāva* and the four Kandy devales, are further differentiated. The Maligava ritual is performed in yearly turns by monks of two different chapters of the Siamese order *(syāmopālivamsika Mahānikāya* or short *Syāma nikāya)* of the Buddhist monkhood *(sangha)* with their headquarters at Malvatta Vihara (*Malvatu vihāraya*, lit. "Flowergarden

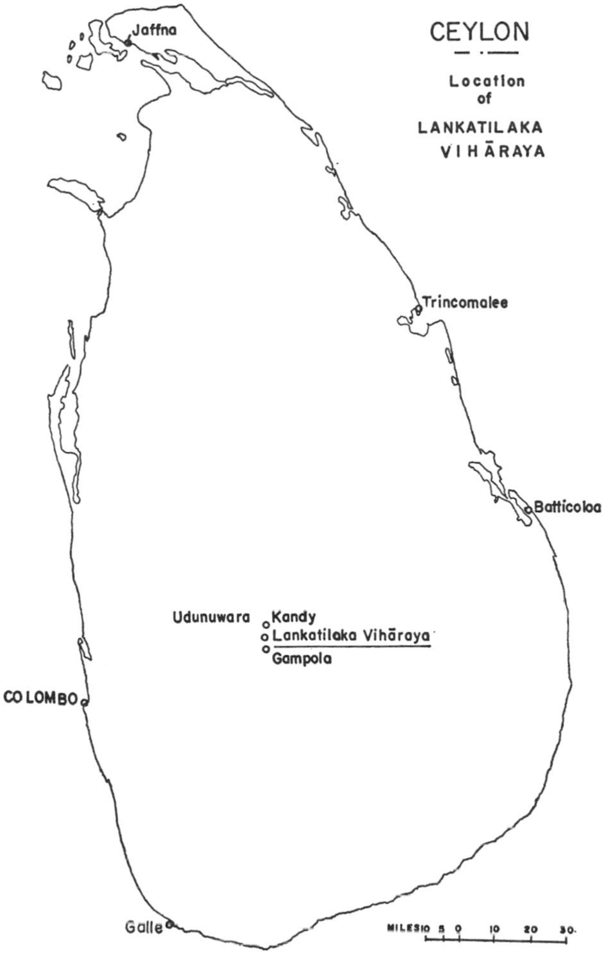

Fig. 1
Map of Ceylon – Location of Lankatilaka Viharaya

Monastery") and Asgiri Vihara (*Asgiri Vihāraya*, lit. "Asgiriya Monastery"). Both are again tied to a great number of other viharas in Central Ceylon, as will be shown later. Similarly each of the devales is loosely connected with other temples dedicated to the worship of the same gods.

The combination and cooperation of the vihara and devale systems in the great Äsala Perahära dates only from the 18th century, when under King Kirti Sri Rajasingha the procession of the Buddha's tooth relic was added to the procession of the four gods. Both systems have, however, existed side by side throughout Ceylonese history. An especially close cooperation was achieved before or during the Gampola period of Ceylonese history in the 14th century and has been challenged only recently in connection with a rationalistic Buddhist modernism. (Ames 1963, Bechert 1966, Chapter IV).

2. The Vihara System

The original meaning of vihara in Pali was dwelling, habitation, place for a convention of bhikkhus, a larger building for housing bhikkhus or an organized monastery. (PTS Dictionary, Dutt 1962: 58). The equivalent in modern Sinhalese, *vihāraya*, has a different meaning: it usually denotes the building or "temple" housing images of the Buddha (also *pilimagē*), whereas the residential quarters of bhikkhus, the "monastery" proper is called *pansala*.[1] Often, however the word *vihāraya* is also used to designate the whole complex of buildings used by bhikkhus for sacred and profane activities. *Vihāraya* is thus a synonym of *sanghārāmaya* or *ārāmaya*. A vihara in this sense will have all or most of the following buildings: there will definitely be a *vihāraya (vihāragē, pilimagē)* with a principal Buddha image, often flanked by two of the Buddha's disciples. It may also contain a *dēvālaya*, a shrine for gods. Some viharas in Central Ceylon are cave temples (e.g. at Dambulla, Hindagalla, or Degaldoruva).

Only the larger and important viharas will have a *pōyagē* which is surrounded by boundary stones *(sīmāgala)* which have been set in an elaborate ceremony to show the limits *(sīmāva)* of a sacred area in which important rituals, *(vinayakarma)* like the higher ordination *(upasampadāva)* or the patimokkha recitation can be performed (Bechert 1961: 21f). Another building is the *banagē* or *banamaduva* where bhikkhus deliver sermons to laymen on poyadays. The poyage is, however, often a multipurpose building which is also used for bana preaching, almsgivings, meetings, and daily offerings to Buddha images *(pūjāva)*. Other sacred places on the vihara compound are stupas *(dāgaba,* also *dāgäba, dāgoba)* which may contain relics, and a wall with small shrines, surrounding a bo tree.

The living quarters of bhikkhus *(pansala)*, traditionally built around a small open courtyard, have a porch in front and a kitchen and a dining hall *(dansalāva)* in the back. Sometimes there is a separate kitchen to prepare the offerings for the Buddha image. A storehouse *(gabadagē)*, a bell tower, a library and a well or bathing pond may complete the outfit of a well equipped vihara.

Some of the buildings, namely the kitchen, dining hall and the storehouse, indicate that most of the bhikkhus no longer make a living by going on pindapata to collect alms, nor is food provided by an almsgivers society *(dayaka sabhāva)*, as in South and Southwestern Ceylon. In fact many viharas own large tracts of land *(vihāragam)* which provided for food and cash income. This system, which Max Weber has aptly termed "monastic landlordism", will be discussed in extenso in a later chapter.[2]

The Dalada Maligava fulfills the function of "temple" *(vihāraya)*; it is not a monastery. The elaborate daily ritual in the two viharas of the Maligava are performed by bhikkhus from Malvatta and Asgiriya taking yearly turns.

---

1 The Pali equivalent of pansala is *paṇṇasālā*, a "hut of leaves." (Rahula 1956:116).
2 See also Bechert 1966, Evers 1964c and SPI 1956.

The Maligava is primarily a pilgrim's place and a symbol of Sinhalese national unity.[1]

Malvatta and Asgiriya Viharas also occupy a special position as they are the two largest monasteries in Central Ceylon. (See Figure 2). Their historical origin is not clear. Bhikkhus from Asgiriya claim a direct connection with a

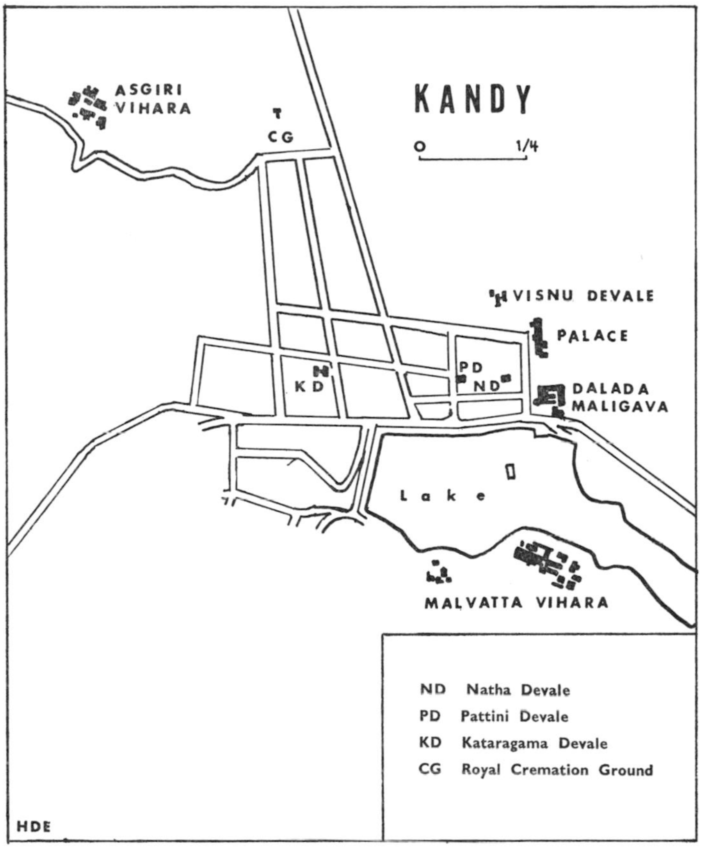

Fig. 2

Map of Kandy, showing the major Temples, Monasteries, and the former Royal Palace

vihara of the same name at Yapavuva north of Kurunegala. When political disturbances broke out they took to the hills in 1312 A.D. and continued the Asgiriya tradition near the present town of Kandy. Tradition has it that a new vihara was built in the time of Bhuvanaikabahu IV of Gampola (1341–1351).[2]

1 Hocart's monograph of the Maligava gives a descriptive account of its architecture, administration and ritual. Hocart 1931.

2 Monks at Asgiri Vihara told me that King Bhuvanaikabahu IV of Gampola (1341–1351) brought five Brahmins over from South India to cure his queen from a disease. They later married Sinhalese women. Two sons of one of these Brahmins, Rama and Ratnapala,

Several informants agreed that Asgiriya was shifted from a former location to the present site by the first king of Kandy, Vimala Dharma Suriya (1591–1604). His queen is said to have donated land to the vihara. In 1753 a party of Thai bhikkhus consecrated a simava at the royal cremation grounds.[1] This act established the Asgiriya ordination tradition of the Siyam Nikaya.

Shortly after an unsuccessful rebellion against Kirti Sri in which bhikkhus from Malvatta were involved (P.E.E. Fernando 1960, Evers 1967), another vihara with sima was constructed by Pilimatalava Adigar I in 1766. His son, Vijasundara Rajakaruna Seneviratna, Pilimatalava Adigar II, had a much larger vihara built at the same compound in 1801. King Sri Vikrama Rajasimha (1798–1815) donated several villages to this Alut Viharaya ("New Temple") and had his gift recorded in a rock inscription *(sannasa)* on the temple wall. The Vijasundararamaya with its new and old vihara became the centre of Asgiriya where all major rituals were performed until in 1827 the present Asgiriya sima was established within the cluster of pansalas in the monastery proper. A new poyage was built in 1948 within these boundaries.

As a consequence of this historical development Asgiriya today consists of three parts: a cluster of about 15 pansalas around the new (1948) poyage and the so-called Mädapansala; the Vijasundararamaya, consisting of two pansalas and two viharas; and the Gedige Viharaya with a pansala.

Malvatta (*Malvatu Vihāraya*, Flowergarden Monastery), then Pusparama (Flower Monastery, Pali *Puppharāma*), was apparently founded by Vimaladhammasuriya I (1592–1604), the first king of Kandy.[2] King Kirti Sri Rajasingha (1747–1781) had a "graceful brick-roofed building erected" here (Mahavamsa 100: 86–87), in which bhikkhus from Thailand ordained Sinhalese novices and thus established the Siyam Nikaya in 1753 (Mahavamsa 100: 91–96, P. E. Pieris 1903).

This building was repaired by King Rajadhirajasimha (1782–1798) according to the Culavamsa (101: 7–11). It has two stories: the lower part is the poyage, which is no longer in use; the upper part is a vihara called Pusparama Viharaya.[3]

The presently used poyage a few hundred yards to the North was built at the end of the 19th century during the Mahanayakaship of Hippola Siri-

were ordained at the new Asgiriya Vihara. One of them supposedly resided in a temple at the present Trinity College grounds which was called Rama Viharaya, the other one at Hantana Viharaya. The Gedige Viharaya south of Asgiriya has indeed some older building elements which resemble the style found at Gadaladeniya Vihara built during Bhuvanaika's reign. Nicholas and Paranavitana (1961: 339) suggest, however, that the Gedige Viharaya was built approximately in the second half of the 15th century. Further research will be necessary to clarify the situation.

1 Apparently shortly after the Malvatta sima was consecrated.

2 It is interesting to note that a monastery in Chiengmai, Northern Thailand, has the same name. This monastery, Wat Sun Dok, was built around 1770 (Credner 1935: 367, LeMay 1926: 80).

3 It contains among other things statues of Kirti Sri Rajasinghe and Vimala Dharma Suriya I and wallpaintings of Välivita Sangharaja and the first 13 Mahanayakas of Malvatta.

Dhammarakkhita Sobhita (1877–1893). The oldest residences of bhikkhus, Välivita Pansala, Tibbotuvave Pansala and Mäde Pansala, were built in the second half of the 18th century and are still used today. Other pansalas were constructed later, so that at present there are 22 pansalas, each owned by a chief incumbent *(vihāradhipati)*.

Malvatta Pansalas

1. Välivita Pansala
2. Tibbatuvāvē Pansala
3. Mäda Pansala
4. Hippola Pansala
5. Galgiriyāvē Pansala
6. Sirimalvatta Pansala
7. Väuda Pansala
8. Madugalla Pansala
9. Telvatta Pansala
10. Haramitigala Pansala
11. Galpihilla Pansala
12. Kulugammana Pansala
13. Pahala Pansala
14. Matgamuvē Pansala
15. Vaṭṭareka Pansala
16. Ambanvälla Pansala
17. Ätulgama Pansala
18. Rambukvälla Pansala
19. Bentara Pansala
20. Pahamuna Pansala
21. Mahanāyaka Pansala
22. Dorēgamuve Pansala

The number of bhikkhus living at Malvatta fluctuates considerably. During *vas*, the time of retreat in the rainy season, there may at times be well over 100 bhikkhus and samaneras (novices) in residence; during the rest of the year only about 50–60 monks.

The simas enclosing the poyage have the same function for the bhikkhus, living at Malvatta, as for a great number of other bhikkhus of the Siyam Nikaya, living all over Ceylon: they all have received their higher ordination *(upasampada)* at the Malvatta sima and their ordination lineages *(paramparāva)* are all originally derived from one of the paramparavas, whose heads occupy and "own" one of the older pansala at Malwatta (Evers 1967). These two aspects are the uniting bonds of the Malwatta chapter of the Siyam Nikaya and distinguish it from the other five chapters of the same order and, of course, from all other nikayas.[1]

It is perhaps misleading to call Malvatta a "monastery," because it is

1 The Sangha of Ceylon is divided into three "orders" *(nikāya)*; the Siyam Nikaya *(siyam* or *syāmanikāya)*, the Amarapura Nikaya *(amarapura nikāya)* and the Ramanya Nikāya *(rāmañña nikāya)*. The Siyam Nikaya is further subdivided into six "chapters," *(pārśvaya)* each of which is headed by a Mahanayake Thero *(mahānāyaka)*. The Amarapura and Ramanya Nikayas are fictional entities, divided into at least 27 and two separate nikayas respectively. The nikayas and chapters have established and maintain a separate tradition of higher ordination *(upasampadā)*.

The process of fission into further nikayas is still going on, officially because of doctrinal disputes, usually on minor vinaya rules. In fact, however, many of the subgroups have been formed either on caste lines, or on account of power struggles within the nikayas. There is no central authority or head of the whole Sangha as the Sangharaja in Thailand. The situation is indeed far more complex than usually assumed in the existing literature, (See Bechert 1966: 211–12, Green 1967, Evers 1967).

rather an agglomeration of independent monasteries. These are the above mentioned 22 pansalas, using a common poyage and common vihares (Pusparama Viharaya and the Dalada Maligava). Each pansala is owned by a chief monk (usually referred to as *loku hāmuduruvo* ("Big Lord") but officially known as *vihārādhipati*). In addition to the *pansala* at Malwatta Vihara each chief monk may control up to seven other temples in the Kandyan Provinces of Central Ceylon (Table 1 and figure 3).

Table 1
Viharas in Central Ceylon

District	*No. of vihāras connected with Malvatta Pansalas*[1]	*Total No. of Vihāras*[2]	*No. of Sinhalese per Vihāra in Hundreds*[3]
Kandy	31	534	9
Kurunegala	20	821	7
Kegalla	4	408	9
Matale	2	116	12
N.I.	6	—	—
	63	1,879	8

Sources:
1 Field notes 1964–66.
2 Buddha ṣāsana Komiśan Vārtāva, S.P. XVIII, 1959.
3 Census 1953.

These viharas account only for about three per cent of all temples located in the same districts. Their importance is, however, much greater than their number might suggest. Most of them are "Great Royal Temples" *(rāja mahā vihāraya)*, or "Ancient Temples" *(purana vihāraya)* which attract crowds of pilgrims and are centres of religious influence and sometimes political power. They often have extensive landholdings which are either worked by tenants on a sharecropping basis or leased to estate companies (mostly tea, rubber, coconut) or held as unrevokable hereditary leases for which service to the temple is due *(rājakāriya)*. (Bechert 1966, SPI 1965, R. Pieris 1956, Evers 1964c, 1967a, 1969a). In any case, the property and the cash income over which the chief priest has control may be high by Ceylonese standards. To cite just one example: the estimated cash income which is probably much lower than the actual total income), of Lankatilaka Vihara *(Lankātilaka rāja mahā vihāraya)*, controlled by the Mahanayaka Thero of Malwatta Vihara was Rs. 22,478.– in 1961/62. The cash income of another temple, owned by the same chief monk, Kobbekaduwa Vihare *(Kobbēkaduva rāja mahā vihāraya)*, was Rs, 10, 196.99 in 1962/63.[1] Even more important, however, is the power and prestige

1 Records of the Public Trustee, Colombo.

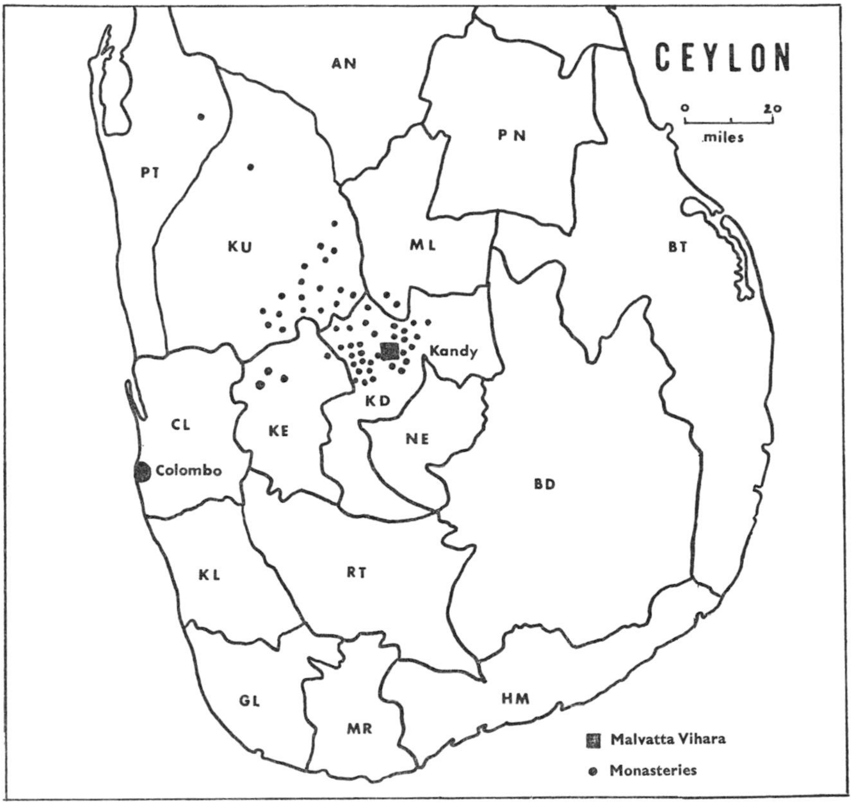

Fig. 3
Monasteries and Monastic Land owned by Chief Monks of Malvatta Vihara, Kandy

Districts

AN	= Anuradhapura District	KU	= Kurunegala District
BD	= Badulla District	KL	= Kalutara District
BT	= Baticaloa District	ML	= Matale District
CL	= Colombo District	MR	= Matara District
GL	= Galle District	NE	= Nuvara Eliya District
HM	= Hambantota District	PN	= Polonnaruva District
KD	= Kandy District	PT	= Puttalam District
KE	= Kegalle District	RT	= Ratnapura District

connected with the ownership of land in Sinhalese society[1] (see table 3 and 4).

Another example might illustrate the interrelation between a Malvatta Pansala and other viharas in Central Ceylon. Välivita Pansala (also: *Śrī Sangharajārāmaya)* at Malvatta was built in the 18th century as residence of Välivita

1 It is therefore quite understandable that considerable importance is attached to the question of succession to the incumbency of temples and the de facto inheritance of temple property. This question is discussed at length in Evers 1967. For the legal aspects see Woodhouse 1917/18, H. W. Tambiah 1962, Wijekulasuriya 1964, Bechert 1966, and Chapter IV of this study.

Saranankara Sangharaja. The present viharadhipati is Välivita Dharmakirti Siri Saranankara Nayaka Thero, who traces his ordination tradition *(paramparā-va)* directly to the Sangharaja. He is also a member of the Sangharajas family and all his predecessors have been close relatives. His teacher, Välivita Asaranasarana Siri Saranankara (Mahanayaka of Malvatta 1955–56), from whom he inherited the pansala, was his father's brother.

The most important temple connected with the Malvatta Välivita Pansala is Gadaladeniya Raja Maha Viharaya in Udunuvara, Kandy District, about 2 miles north of Lankatilaka Temple. The main building, housing a vihara and a devale, was built during the reign of King Bhuvanaikabahu IV of Gampola (1341–1351) and is endowed with considerable landholdings. Its most famous incumbent was Sangharaja Dharmakirti II (14th–15th century), the author of the Nikaya—Sangrahaya and other important Sinhalese works.

Other temples belonging to the same group are the Välivita Pansala at the home village of the last Sangharaja in Tumpane, Kandy District; and in the Kurunegala District, the Algama Raja Maha Vihāraya at Potuhara, the Vatukana Viharaya at Katukota and the Polpitiya Viharaya. Similarly other groups of temples, distributed throughout the Kandyan Provinces, are controlled from pansalas at Malvatta or Asgiriya. There are also other minor temple groups with their own centre. The majority of all other viharas depend, however, on the support of laymen and large temples for their maintenance. This "vihara-system" consequently consists of a network of important temples and a multitude of smaller, more or less dependent viharas.[1]

3. The Devala System

Theravada Buddhism with its major institution, the vihara, has never existed alone in Ceylon. There always have been devales, representing a complimentary religious system. Rahula (1956: 43) claims that temples for gods already existed in the third century B.C. together with the just introduced Buddhist monasteries. In the Buddhist chronicle, the Mahavamsa, devales are frequently mentioned from the fourth century A.D. onwards. (Geiger 1960: 176).

A devale can be a small shrine within a vihara, merely a hut or a large and magnificent building. A typical devale consists of a number of different buildings. The most important part of the main building is the sancta sanctorum containing the image of the god and his weapons. The roof above the shrine room is always topped by a spire and thus easily recognized. The sanctum protected by a curtain from the looks of laymen and only the priest *(kapurāḷa, kapu mahatmaya)* is allowed to enter it after certain purification rituals. A long, open entrance hall *(diggē)* protects drummers, musicians and dancers who

1 In the present discussion regional arrangements and abstract relations have been stressed. The corresponding social relations are discussed in Evers 1967. Comparisons between the organization of Thai and Sinhalese monasteries are found in Evers 1966a and 1966b.

perform their art while the ritual is going on. From the digge a procession street leads through a gateway to the distant procession building (*siṅhāsanaya* or *rittagē*). Somewhere on the devale compound there will be a house where the temple chief (*basnāyaka nilamē*) resides during temple festivals, a kitchen for preparing the offerings (*multängē*), a storehouse (*gabadāgē*) and a small vihara or a bo tree. The kapurala usually lives with his family in an ordinary village house close by.

As Malvatta, Asgiriya and the Dalada Maligava form the center of the vihara system, the four Kandy devales are the focus of the devale system. This system is, however, not as tightly integrated as the vihara system. The connections between the Kandy devales and the outside devales (*piṭisara dēvālaya*) of the same Gods are more of an ideological than social or political nature and imply only few reciprocal duties of priests and temple officials.

The oldest of the four Kandy temples is most probably the Natha Devale, built in the second half of the 14th century. (Nicholas and Paranavitana 1961: 339). Its connection with Buddhism is very close. God Natha has been identified with the Bodhisattva Avalokiteshvara (Bechert 1968: 274) and the dagoba of the vihara on the devale compound is said to contain the Buddha's bowl relic. But it also had other important functions: the Kandyan kings assumed their new royal name here and received their royal sword. The other devales received pots with medicinal plants from this temple for the important *nanumura* ritual which will be discussed in Chapter IV. (Davy 1821: 168). Natha is the only God worshipped at this and all other Natha devales, the most important of which is the Dodanvela Devale in Yatinuvara.

The largest temple, and the richest in terms of temple land, is the Maha Visnu Devala. It is perhaps significant that there is no vihara on the Maha Visnu Devale compound, and one is tempted to speculate that the Dalada Maligava was understood as the Buddhist equivalent to the "Great Vishnu Temple." Like most other Visnu devales, it also features a separate smaller devale for Visnus chief minister (*adigar*) and commander-in-chief Alutnuvara Dädimunda Devata Bandara.

Somewhat less important is the temple of the goddess Pattini, who is more venerated in the low country of Ceylon. Pattini is said to prevent epidemics and to cure smallpox.

The Kataragama Devale is reached through a doorway in between the shops of shoemakers and jewellers in busy Castle Hill Street. The Kapuralas are Tamils from Jaffna, but the Basnayaka Nilame is Sinhalese. To the left of the main building is a pansala in which a bhikkhu of the Malvatta chapter resides. Behind the devale there is a large bo tree and a small vihara. To its right a separate building contains shrines for Gana deviyo (Ganesha), Huniyan Devata, and the Nava Graha (nine planets).

The connection between the four Kandy devales and outer devales is shown in Table 2. It is customary that the temple officials, priests and temple tenants of an outer devale join the procession of their respective Kandy devale during the four festivals, the Äsala Keliya, Karti Mangalaya, Avurudu Manga-

Table 2
Major Devales in Central Ceylon
Kandy devales and connected outer devales

Dēvālaya	*Location*
Kandy Nātha Dēvālaya	Kandy town
(1) Dodanvela D.	Dodanvela, Yatinuvara, Kandy D.
(2) Vegiriya D.	Vegiriya, Udunuvara, Kandy D.
Mahā Visnu Dēvālaya	Kandy town
(1) Lankātilaka D.	Hiyarapitiya, Udunuvara, Kandy District
(2) Gadalādeniya D.	Gadaladeniya, Udunuvara, Kandy District
(3) Hanguranketa D.	Hanguranketa, Uda Hevahata, Nuwara Eliya District
(4) Alavattugoda D.	Alavattugoda, Harispatuva, Kandy District
Kataragama Dēvālaya	Kandy town
(1) Ämbäkka D.	Ä*mb*äkka, Udunuvara, Kandy D.
(2) Ganagoda D.	Ganagoda, Kandy District
Pattini Dēvālaya	Kandy town
(1) Hanguranketa Pattini D.	Hanguranketa, Uda Hävahäta, Nuwara Eliya District

Other important dēvāles:
Kande D., Veravela; Pasgama D.;
Valahagoda D., Kotmale Pattini D.

laya and Alutsal Mangalaya. Otherwise there seem to be no further official ties. (Table 2 and Figure 4).

Similarly to the vihara system, the devale system also has more or less independent units which are, however, of lesser importance. They usually have no temple land, often not even a professional kapurala, and attract few devotees. An exemption is perhaps the Kandy Devale in Udunuvara, which has temple lands, but no Basnayaka Nilame, is managed and owned by a kapurala and attracts large crowds for its festivals.

So far we have tried to analyse the vihara and the devale systems separately. In reality, especially from the point of view of the Sinhalese villager, both systems work closely together, as already shown in our short description of the Kandy perahära. The close interconnection between the vihara and the devale systems is also evident from its regional organization. The religious center of Ceylon is, at least from an upcountry-Sinhalese point of view, the town of Kandy with the Temple of the Tooth *(Daḷadā Māḷigāva)* and the temples of the four guardian deities Visnu, Natha, Kataragama and Pattini. But each of these deities has its own realm where it is supposed to be most powerful and where it has a principal temple. There are also other purely Buddhist centres of worship and pilgrimmage, challenging the dominance of Kandy. The most prominent is the ancient city of Anuradhapura, which has acquired new prominence in the wake of rising Sinhalese Buddhist nationalism. Similarly the

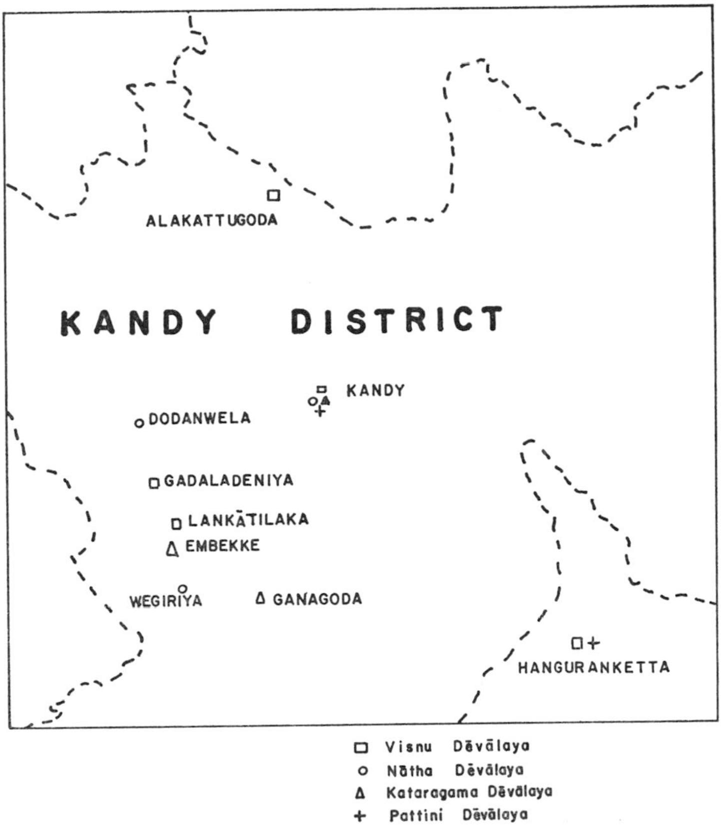

Fig. 4
Major Devales, Kandy District

devale of Kataragama in Southeastern Ceylon has emerged as the most popular pilgrim center of all Sinhalese gods. (Obeyesekere 1966: 25, Wirz 1954b).

4. The Palace System

The royal palace in Kandy *(māḷigāva)* represented a third "religious" system before the Sinhalese kingdom was abolished in 1815. The king in Ceylon similar to the ruler in other Indian and Southeast Asian empires was regarded as a divine person, a *dēvarāja* and at times as a future Buddha, a *Bōdhisattva*. Thus the king, the Buddha and the gods formed a religious community which merged in the person of the king himself to a lesser or greater degree.

Thus the king has at certain times been called a *dēvā* not necessarily in the sense of "God", but as "one of a class of powerful beings, regarded as possessing supernormal faculties and as controlling a department of nature or activity in the human sphere" (Gonda 1966: 24). The king was in this sense not an incarnation of one particular god, but one of the community of gods and godlings in his own right. At other times and in other contexts the king as *dēvārāja* was understood as "identical with all gods or all the divinities" (Gonda 1966: 24). In other cases still a king expressly claimed to be an incarnation of a specific god, as Heine-Geldern has pointed out (1956: 6). King Airlangga of Java (11th Century) was an incarnation of both Visnu and Buddha; Suryavarnam II of Cambodia (12th Century), the builder of Angkor Vat, is regarded as an incarnation of Visnu; and Krtarajasa (14th century), the founder of the Majapahit empire claimed to be an incarnation of both Siva and Visnu. Recently Coedes has advanced another interpretation. He says that in ancient Cambodia the *dēvāraja* was not the person of the divine king himself, but the permanent principle and the essence of kingship, which identified itself with the soul of successive rulers. (Coedes 1951: 141). The essence of kingship was understood to reside in an image of a god or a lingam and had to be animated by a special rite (Gonda 1966: 61).

From these remarks (and, of course, from the full texts from which these remarks were drawn) we can subtract a basic principle of this cultural theme: The power of the king rested on his *identification* with a god. The identification could be more or less close, the king could just be compared to a god or he could be seen as his incarnation. "Identification" is thus a variable, not a constant.

This basic principle was not changed by the influence of Mahayana or Theravada Buddhism in Southeast Asia and Ceylon. The identification with a god in varying degrees was not given up, but supplemented by an again changing degree of identification with a Buddha. Burmese and Sinhalese kings have at times claimed to be Bodhisatvas or even Buddhas themselves. Their high status emenated from their good *kamma* and their religious merit gained through gifts to the Buddhist monkhood and the performance of elaborate Buddhist ritual. Thus in Buddhist countries Bodhisatva, god and king became a triangle of mutual identification. In Ceylon gods and kings were seen as future Buddhas, Bodhisatvas were venerated as gods, the king as devaraja and Bodhisatva. The respective personnel of the three units, Buddhist monks, Brahmin priests and court officials, became the major social and political forces around which the fate of the societies revolved. Their respective institutions and organizations—temples for the Buddha, temples for the gods and palaces for the king—became merged at certain times in the history of Southeast Asia and Ceylon or gained more or less power over each other. The Sanskrit term *prasada* was used to denote a temple as the seat and dwelling of divine power and also to describe a royal residence (Gonda 1966: 54); the Sinhalese term *māḷigāva* was used both for the temple of the Buddha's tooth relic and for the royal palace. Often, as will be noted below, the three institutions and superhuman beings were glued together by parallel rituals of identification. The period of the greatest integration and identification of the three parts of the cultural complex of Buddha, god and king was probably the 12th–14th century. In Indonesia kings were seen as incarnations of Siva-Buddha and the syncretism between the formerly separate traditions was completely accepted

(Stoehr and Zoetmulder 1965: 270). In this period the contact between Ceylon and Indonesia was very intense, as Paranavitana has discussed in his book on "Ceylon and Malaysia" (1966). Perhaps due to Southeast Asian influences even in Ceylon, the center of orthodox Theravada Buddhism, temples were built incorporating shrines for both the Buddha and the gods, as the Lankatilaka temple to be described in detail later on. Thus the capitals of the late Sinhalese kingdoms, including the last one of Kandy, were built around a spatially and ritually closely integrated complex of temples for the gods, the Buddha and a palace for the king. In close proximity we find in the centre of the city the royal palace surrounded by the Buddhist temple (the Dalada Maligava), the temple of Visnu (Maha Visnu Devalaya) and the temples of the other guardian deities of Ceylon. (See figure 2). All three types of establishments were, and still are, centres of an elaborate system of officials, rituals and landed properties with the appropriate tenants and servants.

The great yearly festivals, the perahäras, eventually became gigantic joint rituals of identification and integration of the Buddha, the gods and the government before the colonial powers destroyed the monarchy and supplemented their secular administration for the divine kingship of old. The king has gone, but the Buddha and the gods remained as unbalanced parts of a system which had evolved through more than two milleniums. The political struggle which ensued in Ceylon in the 1950's should also be seen in this perspective. Political demands for the restoration of Buddhism to "its rightful place" as well as for the Singhalization of Government are all endeavors to restore the balance, to find a new social and political variation on an ancient cultural theme.

Though the king is no longer there in reality, he still looms large in the minds of Sinhalese villagers. References to "the days of the Sinhalese kings" are often made. History and myth are not dead but an integral part of everyday life. In addition to this "historical reality," the Kandyan aristocracy is still important and continues the royal tradition. Radala families continue to live in their manors *(valavva)* and occupy high religious and political offices.

5. The Economic Base: Control over Land and Services

The vihara, devale and palace systems derived their stability to a large extent from their economic base, namely the ownership of land and the control over services.[1] Though all land was, according to the traditional state ideology, owned by the king, his effective control was severely curtailed by the vihara and devale systems. The Kandyan king could still deprive Kandyan nobles of their official lands (*nindagam*) and the service of nindagam tenants, but templelands *(vihāragam* and *dēvālagam)* could not be alienated as they were technically donated to and owned by higher authorities, the Buddha and his monkhood and the Gods.

1 The following section draws heavily on Evers 1969a.

This temple land system which was termed "monastic landlordism" by Max Weber (1958: 257) and "Buddhist temporalities" by British officials, has survived the onslaught of British colonialism more or less by default, has regained strength and importance with the economic development of the Ceylon up-country, and is now a major focus of Kandyan Sinhalese social structure maintaining the feudal aristocracy, perpetuating caste distinctions, stalling reforms of the Sangha and playing a distinctive role in nationalist politics.

The driving force behind the historical development of the temple land system was the desire of Buddhist laymen to earn "merit" by donating land to the Sangha. The first land grant is reported in a Sinhalese Chronicle as far back as the first century B.C. (Mahavamsa 33: 38ff). Especially with the growing power of the Buddhist god-king in a "hysraulic society" the legitimization through merit-gaining donations became more and more important. (Evers 1963). Towards the end of the Anuradhapura period in the 10th Century A.C. Buddhist monasteries must have owned a fair proportion of all irrigated rice-lands. The administration of Buddhist monasteries and monastic property was, however, highly rationalized and bureaucratized during this period and the term "monastic landlordism" is not yet appropriate.[1]

In fact, "monastic capitalism" might be more useful to characterize the social and economic organization of large monasteries at that time. Accounts were kept and regularly audited, many lay officials and servants of the monasteries were paid in cash (gold), and interest from capital endowments were used to maintain monk scholars and monastic establishments very much in the same way American Ivy League Universities are operated today.[2] Frequent warnings against private use of monastic property found in stone inscriptions indicate, however, inherent dangers and future developments. An attempt to secure control over temple property by individual monks is also evidenced by the emergence of a "rule of pupilary succession" which is mentioned for the first time in a 10th century stone inscription.[3] This rule, which regulates the inheritance of monastic property today, gives an "owner" of a monastery the right to determine his successor and heir to the monastic property. The appropriation of monastic property by individual monks and the transmission of this property from pupil to pupil within the same family along an ordination lineage *(paramparāva)* created from the late Polonnaruva up to the Kandyan period the system which most appropriately might be called "monastic landlordism." Donations of land were not only made to Buddhist monasteries (the "vihara system") but also to temples of deities (the "devale system"). The interrelation between both types of land *(vihāragam* and *dēvālagam)* will occupy our attention at great length later on.

---

1 Max Weber is perhaps not to be blamed in this case. His term "Klostergrundherrschaft" does not convey the same meaning as "monastic landlordism", namely that there is an individual, a landlord, who owns land and commands tenants.

2 See e.g. the Tablets of Mahinda IV, 956–972 A.C., *Epigraphia Zeylanica*, Vol. 1 (1904–12), pp. 75–113 and other inscriptions. The system is descriped in Rahula 1956.

3 Buddhannehäla Pillar Inscription, *Epigraphia* Zeylanica, Vol. 1 (1904–12), pp. 191–200.

That "monastic landlordism" has survived up to the present, despite all the forces of change which have swept Ceylon since that fatal morning in 1505 when a Portuguese ship appeared on her shores, is due to two major mistakes or miscalculations. The first were made by King Kirti Sri Rajasingha (1747–1780) who helped to revive Buddhism by reintroducing the ordination tradition from Thailand. A history of the Kandyan Kingdom has not yet been written and the following thought is therefore nothing more than a tentative hypothesis: Kirti Sri, a king of South Indian origin, tried to strengthen the Buddhist Sangha in order to weaken the Sinhalese aristocracy. The Sangha was, however, quickly "infiltrated" by the Kandyan aristocracy, and monastic landlords *(vihārādhipati)* gained power with the accumulation of lands, donated or redonated by the king. An attempt in 1760 to assassinate the king in the Malvatta monastery during a religious ceremony made his miscalculation apparent.[1] (P. E. E. Fernando 1960, *Sāsanāvatīrna varnanāva*, British Museum Oriental Ms Collection Or 6606/12).

Kirti Sri Rajasingha had thus strengthened monastic landlordism and with it unwillingly the Kandyan aristocracy and the Kandyan caste system. Another misjudgment hindered the destruction of monastic landlordism during the 19th century: Christian missionaries brought pressure on the British government to avoid interference with matters concerning the "idolatrous system of religion in Ceylon." It was argued that Buddhism would collapse and Christian missionary efforts triumph, if only the pledge of the Kandyan Convention of 1815 would be broken and government protection withdrawn. The colonial administration adjusted its policies accordingly. (Evers 1964b). The long term results were, however, not anticipated: the reforms abolishing the Kandyan feudal administration in the 1830's exempted the religious sphere. Consequently monastic landlordism not only survived but was strengthened. Lack of government control made widespread "corruption," that is further appropriation and personal use of temple lands by individual monks and temple lords, possible. The colonial government eventually intervened in the latter part of the 19th century by appointing a temple land commission. As Buddhist nationalists have bemoaned ever since, the registration of temple lands and temple services deprived the temples of claims to about half their lands. On the other hand, the system for the first time was systematically formalized and put down in writing with the result that "monastic landlordism" was officially recognized, stabilized and strengthened by colonial law enforcement agencies.[2]

Two major miscalculations of the then ruling powers thus made it possible that a part of Kandyan feudal organization survived its eclipse, and continued

1 One is tempted to draw comparisons with the assassination of Prime-Minister S.W.R.D. Bandaranaike in 1959. In both cases an alliance between a chief monk of an important monastery and high ranking government officials was formed with the intention to murder the head of the government who happened in both cases to be a strong supporter of Buddhism and Buddhist revival.

2 In contrast to the position taken here the actions of the British Government are usually seen as highly destructive for Buddhism and the Buddhist Sangha. So e.g. in Tennakoon Vimalananda 1963.

to function as a vestige of traditional values in modern Ceylon. I shall now have a brief look at "monastic landlordism" in presentday Central Ceylon.

The extent of land owned by Buddhist monasteries in Ceylon is difficult to ascertain, an accurate figure has never been compiled. I would estimate that there are some 135,000 acres viharagam in Central Ceylon (by Central Ceylon is meant the formerly Kandyan provinces, see table 3), and that about 10 per cent of all paddy land in this area is viharagam.[1]

Table 3

Distribution of Viharagam, Dēvālagam and Nindagam in Ceylon: Paraveni panguvas subject to rājakāriya

District	*Vihāragam*		*Dēvālagam*		*Nindagam*	
	Villages No.	*Extent a–p–k*	*Villages No.*	*Extent a–p–k*	*Villages No.*	*Extent a–p–k*
Kandy	226	1,817–3–6	58	989–2–3	9	36–0–8
Matale	54	1,830–1–4	9	276–0–5	69	443–0–5
Nuwara Eliya	9	157–3–9	23	476–3–2	1	18–1–8
Kegalla	35	714–3–2	80	2,296–1–6	93	2,376–3–5
Kurunegala	132	3,235–1–9	152	2,970–3–4	4	292–2–7
Badulla	29	179–3–4	144	1,325–3–1	90	1,303–1–5
Ratnapura	12	1,361–0–9	46	4,378–0–0	127	7,457–0–2
Anuradhapura	46	229–0–3	5	16–2–5	118	409–2–0
Polonnaruwa	2	70–3–5	—	—	—	—
Matara	1	55–2–3	—	—	—	—
Total	546	9,653–0–4	517	12,730–0–6	511	12,337–1–0

Source: Sessional Paper I, 1956, pp. 28–29. *Note*: a–p–k see Chapter V:5.

Percentage Distribution of Temple Lands

District	*Viharagam p.c.*	*Devalagam p.c.*	*Area of Districts p.c.*
Kandy	19	8	8
Matale	19	2	7
Nuwara Eliya	2	4	4
Kegalla	7	18	6
Kurunegala	33	23	16
Badulla	2	10	9
Ratnapura	14	34	11
Anuradhapura	2	1	23
Polonnaruwa	1	0	12
Matara	1	0	4
	100	100	100

1 These figures are based on a rough evaluation of materials collected in the Ceylon Government Archives and the Record Room of the Kandy Kachcheri. One major difficulty was the recalculation of Sinhalese landmeasures whose acre-equivalent changes from district to district.

Viharagam as part of the vihara system, is land attached to Buddhist monasteries (e.g. the well-known Ridi Vihara or Lankatilaka Vihara) or temples (e.g., the Temple of the Tooth in Kandy). A somewhat higher acreage of land, the *dēvālagam*, belongs to temples of Sinhalese gods and forms part of the devale system. There are two basic categories of temple lands, usually referred to as *baṇḍāra* lands and as *paravēni pangu*. Bandara lands are owned by a particular monastery *(vihāraya)* and are controlled by its chief monk or incumbent. The chief monk *(vihārādhipati)* farms out these lands to sharecroppers on three year contracts, has them worked by temple servants, or in the case of some highlands rents them to tea, rubber or coconut estates on long term leases. Some estates are directly managed by chief monks who hire overseers and teapluckers or rubbertappers and sell their products to tea or rubber factories. The income from these lands does not accrue to the Buddhist order of monks *(Saṅgha)* or the Buddhist church, but to the individual monastery and its chief monk. Though in the case or larger monasteries and temples estimates of income and expenditure have to be submitted to the Public Trustee in Colombo, effective financial control is not exercised. Income from bandara lands can therefore be used for capital formation and investment in business enterprises or political campaigns, as well as for religious festivals or temple renovation. The excessive use of monastic income for business ventures and political campaigns is, for example, documented in the proceedings of the Bandaranaike murder case against Buddharakkhita Thero, a chief monk of the Kelaniya Vihara (Smith 1966: 498, Bechert 1966:344, Evers 1964a: 102).

The extent of modern "monastic capitalism" is difficult to assess. There are at least 24 monasteries and Buddhist temples with a declared annual income of over 10,000 Rs. Their combined income ran to 717,754.07 Rs. in 1963. (see Table 4 and 5).

The chief monks *(vihārādhipati)* of major monasteries and the temple lords *(basnāyaka nilamē)* of large devales are therefore extremely powerful. They are landlords controlling large tracts of land, accumulating considerable funds and having authority over many monks, priests and peasants. All chief monks in Central Ceylon belong to the Goyigama caste, and many of them to the Radala subcaste, the Kandyan aristocracy. Together with the temple lords *(basnāyaka nilamē)* of the devales, almost all of whom are Radala, and other landlords they perpetuate the Kandyan feudal system. Their operation in Ceylon national politics is "traditional"—through personal relations, kinship and marriage within the modern framework of political parties and parliamentary democracy. The kinship network of Mrs. Sirimavo Bandaranaika, Prime Minister of Ceylon, 1960–1964 and 1970 might serve as an example. She is a born Ratwatte (a prestigious Radala family), and owns large estates herself. Her father, who had the title of disava (Kandyan Provincial Governor), and one of her brothers served as chiefs of the richest Buddhist temple, the Dalada Maligava in Kandy. Another brother is the Public Trustee, whose fuction is, among other things, the supervision of temples and their properties; still another brother held a seat in the fourth and fifth parliaments. She is related

Table 4

Buddhist Monasteries and Temples with a Declared Annual Cash Income of Rs. 10,000 and more, 1962–63

	Rs.
1. Srīpādaṣtānaya (Adam's Peak)	182,929.48
2. Kolavenigama Rāja Mahā Vihāraya	65,811.18
3. Kiriälla Nädun Vihāraya	51,716.49
4. Srī Daḷadā Māḷigāva (Temple of the Tooth)	58,214.67
5. Tissamahārāma Vihāraya	35,671.39
6. Rajōpavanarāmaya, Peradeniya	31,719.61
7. Kälani Rāja Mahā Vihāraya	28,948.62
8. Mahiyangana Rāja Mahā Vihāraya	23,829.88
9. Papiliyana Rāja Mahā Vihāraya	21,749.12
10. Dambulla Rāja Mahā Vihāraya	20,289.34
11. Niyangampāya Vihāraya	17,579.36
12. Pusulpitiya Vihāraya	16,017.69
13. Degaldoruva Rāja Mahā Vihāraya	17,072.29
14. Aṭamaṣthanaya (Anuradhapura)	16,480.64
15. Maddevela Rāja Mahā Vihāraya	15,906.00
16. Bingiriya Vihāraya	15,818.22
17. Huduhumpola Vihāraya	14,194.10
18. Mutiyangana Rāja Māha Vihāraya	14,040.72
19. Yatala Manik Vihāraya	13,387.43
20. Rambukpota Rāja Mahā Vihāraya	12,601.47
21. Khettarāma Kande Vihāraya	11,878.01
22. Ridi Vihāraya	11,069.82
23. Budumuttāva Rāja Mahā Vihāraya	10,631.55
24. Kobbēkaduva Vihāraya	10,196.99
Total	717,754.07

Source: Administration Report of the Public Trustee for 1962–63, B.S.C. Ratwatte, Esq., Colombo: Government Press, 1964.

Table 5

Declared Income of Four Major Buddhist Temples, 1934–1963 (in Rs.)

	1934	*1938*	*1963*
Srī Daladā Māligāva	17,892.83	19,207.64	58,214.67
Lankātilaka Vihāraya	13,413.56	13,333.45	22,478.00
Nädun Vihāraya	10,600.67	13,764.92	51,716.49
Ridi Vihāraya	6,832.52	6,027.54	11,069.82

Source: Public Trustee, Administration Reports.

to the Governor General of Ceylon, to the Mahanayaka Thero of Malwatta Vihara, the largest monastery in Ceylon, and to most of the other important Kandyan Radala families.

Generally the "monastic landlords" of Central Ceylon have tended to remain in the background and abstain, for example, from attendance at political mass meetings. The Mahanayaka Theros of Malwatta and Asgiriya have often voiced their disapproval of the activities of "political monks", operating primarily in the low country.[1] Their political activities have tended to follow traditional practices: private meetings with those in power, exploitation of kinship connections or rivalries, personal favours and subsidies.

The values and ideologies underlying temple landlordism can best be seen in the operation of the service tenure system *(rājakāriya)* of Buddhist monasteries and temples in Central Ceylon, which will be analysed in detail in Chapter V.

A temple or feudal estate *(vihāragama, dēvālagama* or *nindagama)* consists of several shares *(panguva)*, the estates of the larger temples can have more than a hundred. The *paravēni pangus* are plots of land of varying size and at the same time units of services. They are owned by peasants who can mortgage, inherit or sell the land. Whoever owns a paraveni panguva is, however, liable to perform temple services *(rājakāriya)* under the direction of the chief monk, the temple lord or the feudal lord respectively. The services and their money values are laid down in the service tenure register of 1872, which is the basis of the present system. Landlords can sue tenants for non-performance of services on the basis of this register but this is seldom done today and many services are no longer performed. Often the chief monks have, however, established a very effective system of control by renting bandara lands to holders of paraveni pangus. Nonperformance of services can then be sanctioned by eviction from bandara lands. In the case of nindagam, services due to the landlord were rarely performed in most cases in 1964–66. The nindagam lords made use only of the *muttețțuva* part of the nindagam, which they owned in full. The remnants of the nindagam system were abolished in 1970, when the Nindagam Ordinance of 1968 was put into operation.

Some pangus of the *vihāragama* or *dēvālagama*, often five, make up the gam-vasama or land of temple officials. The tenants of these lands have to act as messengers, overseers over the cultivation of temple fields *(muttețțuva)*, measurers of rice and supervisors of the monastic granary, etc. All of them are members of the goyigama caste, frequently of families of the former Kandyan petty bureaucracy.

The other pangus belong to the *nilavasama* or servant's land. The temple servants *(nilakāriyā)* are drawn from all the major Sinhalese castes. Their services, performed during the four annual festivals and during the daily rituals, reflect their caste status. The ritual in the temples of the large landowning monasteries and in the Temple of the Tooth in Kandy is very elaborate, requires the daily attendance of many temple servants, and differs considerably

1 The Council of the Malvatta Monastery in Kandy officially condemned political activities of monks in 1946. See Heinz Bechert, 1966: 313. The present Mahanayaka of Malvatta also declared that monks should abstain from politics (*World Buddhism*, Vol. 12, No. 10 (1946), pp. 23–24). This does not mean that he himself did not try to influence the government. His "political style" is indicated by his demand to have an official residence in Colombo, the capital. This demand was partly filled by giving him the former residence of a high colonial official in Kandy.

from the often described and admired simplicity of Buddhist ritual in smaller temples. These rituals will be described later in Chapter IV, but we might mention that they are in their basic structure identical with the ritual in the temples of the gods *(dēvālaya)* and with the former royal ritual in the Kandyan palace. That means that until 1815 monastic estates, temple estates and royal estates supported identical rituals of purification and annointment performed daily before the Buddha, the Gods and the King. The palace ceremonial has ceased, but the ritual in the viharas and devales is still going on without cessation stressing the unity of the Buddha, Gods and Government.

Temple landlordism is certainly a mixed blessing for Ceylon. In its service tenure system caste distinctions are emphasized and perpetuated and members of the "bhikkhu Sangha", the fraternity of beggars, are among the richest landlords of Central Ceylon, closely tied in with Kandyan aristocratic families. Reforms of the Buddhist Sangha and land reforms—both urgently needed—are effectively stalled.

The "monastic landlords" of Central Ceylon have successfully protested against the implementation of the recommendations of the Buddhist Committee of Inquiry of 1955 which had mildly criticized the role of pupilary succession and the transmission of monastic property to blood relatives. (Buddhist Commision of Inquiry 1956, Wriggins 1960: 195, Bechert 1966: 269). They opposed the Buddha Sasana Commision of 1959 which recommended that viharagam should be centrally administered by an appointed official, and they threatened in 1963, through the Diyavadana Nilame, the head of the Temple of the Tooth, to close the temple and stop the ritual if land reform was to be extended to monastic and temple lands as well.

To understand the dynamics of Theravada Buddhism as a social and political force in modern Ceylon, a knowledge of the traditional base of its power and stability over centuries, the temples and monasteries, is imperative.

The following chapters will be concerned with a detailed analysis of the social, religious and economic organization of one particular temple in Central Ceylon. This detailed analysis will, it is hoped, lead to a better understanding of the traditions and dynamics of Theravada Buddhism and Buddhist societies.

CHAPTER TWO

Lankatilaka: Introduction to a Royal Temple

1. The Great Royal Temple and Monastery

ŚRI *Lankātilaka Raja Maha Vihāraya*, the "Radiant Great Royal Temple of Lankatilaka," towers on a steep rock in the centre of the Udunuvara Division, about half-way between the old royal cities of Kandy and Gampola (Figure 5). A small footpath runs through the paddy fields in the valley, then up the hill through a temple owned plantation of palmtrees to the monastery. From there one has to climb the ancient stairs hewn into the bare rock until one reaches the main gate of the temple proper. Only two stories of the 14th century structure have survived a Portuguese raid in the 17th century. These are covered with several tiled roofs. Originally the temple had 4 stories and must have looked more like a Javanese temple than like its 12th century predecessor and namesake in Polonnaruva, one of the centres of the ancient Sinhalese empire in Northern Ceylon. In fact, experts agree that the architecture of Lankatilaka is very much influenced by Southeast Asian, possibly Burmese models (Mudiyanse n.d.: 68–69; Hocart 1926: 18–20; Paranavitana 1960– 784). Local monks claim that the neighbouring temple of Gadaladeniya was built at the same time by a Burmese architect from Amaravati.

The main entrance, under a huge *makara torana*, leads through two antechambers into the Buddhist shrine room, the *vihāraya*. A colossal seated Buddha, surrounded by a relief of celestial beings and flanked by two standing Buddhas, is the principal image of the temple. The vihara is, however, encircled by a corridor, which cannot be entered from the vihara, but through five doors in the outer temple wall (see figure 7). Each door leads to a small shrine *(dēvālaya)* in the inner wall of the temple. These five shrines, as well a sixth one which has been added later, contain images of Gods and their consorts. The Buddha is thus surrounded by six Gods facing the cardinal directions. This demonstrates vividly that the Gods have to protect the Buddha and his teachings according to Sinhalese believes. Four of the doors normaly remain closed. The devale is entered through an open hall *(diggē)* and the door exactly opposite the main entrance to the vihara.

This very close connection between vihara and devale, housing under one roof a shrine for the Buddha and shrines for the gods, is unique and is found only in a limited number of temples. Another better-known example is the temple at Gadaladeniya situated a few miles North of Lankatilaka and built

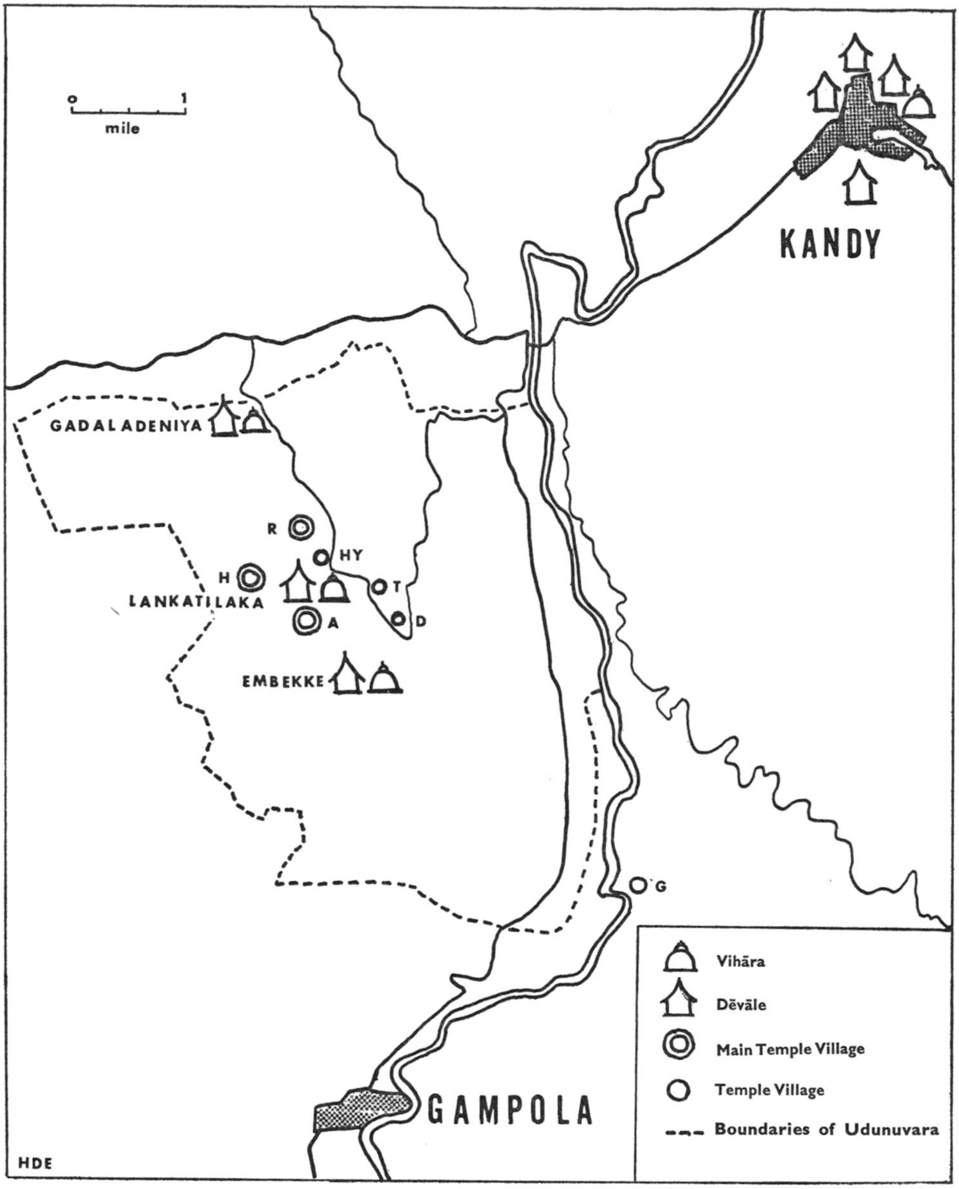

Fig. 5

Lankatilaka and its Temple Villages

H = Hiddaula (Dēvālagam)	T = Tirappuva
R = Rabbegamuva (Vihāragam)	D = Daulagalle
A = Arawwawala (Vihāragam)	G = Godawela
HY = Hiyarapitiya	

in the same period. Most viharas in Central Ceylon have, however, one or more images of gods, a small shrine for a god or a separate devale on their premises; and similarly most devales have a small vihara attached to them.

From the main gate of the devale a procession alley *(perahära vīdiya)* des-

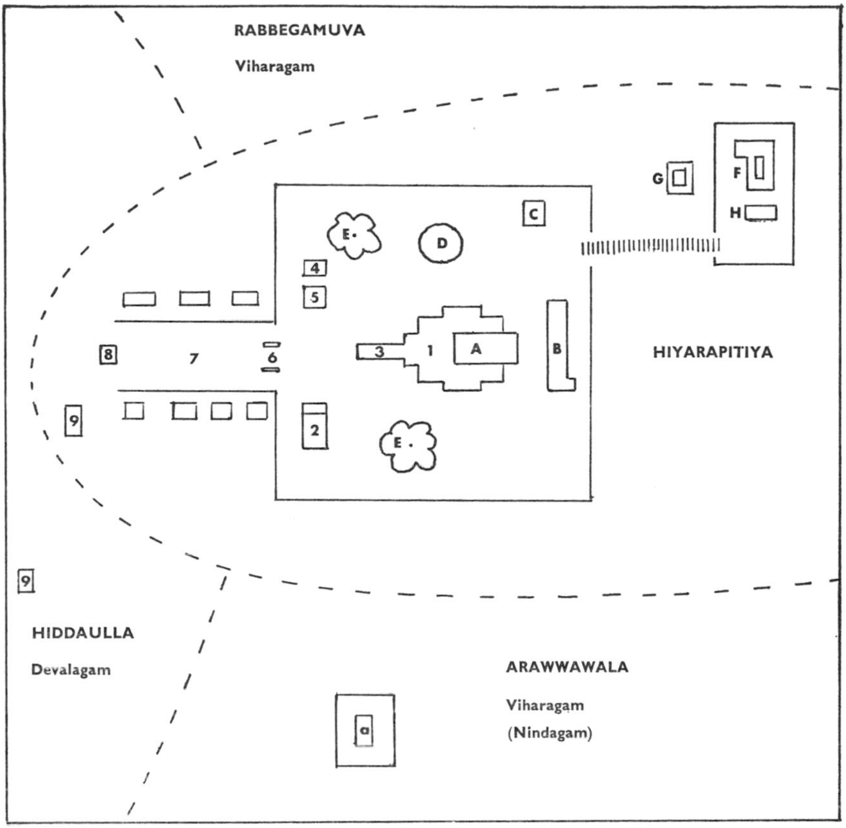

Fig. 6

The Lankatilaka Temple Compound (not drawn to scale)

Vihāra System

A. Temple of the Buddha *(vihāraya)*
B. Hall of drummers *(diggē)* and kitchen for offerings *(multängē)*
C. Preaching house *(banagē)*
D. Relic mound *(dagoba)*
E. Bo-trees
F. Monastery *(pansala)*
G. Assembly hall *(poyagē)* and sacred boundary *(sīmāva)*
H. Paddy store house of the monastery *(gabadagē)*

Dēvāle System

1. Temple of the gods *(dēvālaya)*
2. Temple of Däḍimuṇḍa Dēvata Baṇḍāra
3. Hall of drummers *(diggē)*
4. Kitchen for offerings *(multängē)*
5. Resthouse of temple lord *(basnāyaka nilamē)*
6. Temple gate *(vahalkaddē)*
7. Procession street *(perahära vīdiya)*
8. Procession house *(sinhāsena)*
9. Houses of priests *(kapurāla)*

Palace System

a. Manor *(valavva)*

— — — village boundaries

cends, through a now ruined entrance hall *(vahalkaḍa)*, to the procession house *(sinhāsanaya)*. Its door is about 7 feet above ground to allow the priests to board their elephants in comfort during the annual procession *(perahära)*. There are a number of other buildings belonging to the devale complex of the temple. In the southwestern corner of the temple compound is a small separate devale, dedicated to a minor god, and behind it a place where offerings to spirits and demons are made from time to time. (See figure 6). In the northwestern corner we find two small mud huts. One serves as the kitchen where offerings for the gods are prepared *(multängē)*, the other as the "residence" of the temple lord *(Basnayaka Nilamē)* during the annual procession. The priests of the devale live in ordinary village houses in a village west of Lankatilaka.

The vihara complex is more elaborate. There are two huge bo trees of the kind under which the Buddha is said to have found his enlightenment, a dagoba (relic mount) north of the main temple building, a one-room preaching hall *(banagē)*, and a long tileroofed building opposite the vihara gate. The middle of this building *(diggē)* is open on two sides and allows a breathtaking view over the valleys and hills of the Kandyan upcountry. The temple musicians play here during the daily rituals. The hall is flanked on one side by the storeroom and on the other side by the small shrine room *(vihāraya)*, which contains a number of small bronze images of the Buddha. In an annex behind the shrine are the kitchen for offerings *(multängē)* and a room where the officiating monk can rest.

The monastery *(pansala)* itself is situated on a small plateau halfway down the temple hill. The view of the main building is obstructed by a large barn where the harvest from the monastic paddy fields is stored. The prominence of this grain storehouse *(gabaddāgē)* impresses even upon the most casual visitor that the monastery is not only the abode of meditating monks following relentlessly the path to nirvana but also the centre of a large estate and the seat of a monastic landlord.

The monastery *(pansala)* is built around a small courtyard from which heavy wooden doors lead to eight rooms on two sides. The tiled roof rests on a row of pillars around the inner court and forms an inner veranda on one side. There is a small table with a tray on which the usual implements for chewing betel are displayed, a diwan on which the senior monks like to rest, a number of armchairs and two miniature chairs which ensure that important visitors are seated, but lower than any of the monks. The *pansala* is entered through a roomy varanda from which the monks can watch villagers and pilgrims climb the temple hill and where some monastic ceremonies, like giving food to the monks to gain religious merit *(dāna)*, are performed. The back of the monastery is occupied by the eating hall *(dansalāva)* and the kitchen *(dangē)*. By and large the monastery resembles the residence of a member of the Sinhalese aristocracy *(valavva)*.

Behind the pansala there is a well surrounded by a high wall, a power house with a diesel generator providing illumination for the main temple on Buddhist holidays, and, a few steps up the hill, a small *pōyagē*. This hall of rites is an essential attribute of any important monastery though it is hardly ever used at Lankatilaka. The building is surrounded by a low wall and by six boundary stones marking the limits *(sīmāva)* in which formal meetings of the order, higher ordinations *(upasampadāva)* and recitations of the rules of conduct for monks *(pāthimokha)* can be held. All these functions are now performed at the Malvatta Monastery in Kandy, with which Lankatilaka is affiliated.

We might pause here for a moment and summarize our descriptive account of the Lankatilaka temple complex (Figure 6). The main building is divided between a temple for the Buddha *(vihāraya)* and a temple for the gods *(dēvālaya)*. Attached to either section are a number of other buildings most of which serve parallel functions: there are two halls of drummers *(dīggē)*, two kitchens *(multängē)* and there are the residence of the Buddhist monks and the houses of the priests of the gods. In addition to the two sections of the temple complex there is a third, complementary one, which has somewhat declined in importance during the past century but is still essential for an understanding of the total system. This section comprises the manors *(valavva)* of the Kandyan aristocracy and formerly the royal palace *(māḷigāva)*.

There are three valavvas in the vicinity of Lankatilaka. One is situated just below the temple on the other side of a small valley south of the temple rock. It was built in the 1920's and its owner lives as absentee landlord in Kandy. The other two are more ancient and are found in the village of Arawawwala just south of Lankatilaka. The old manor is reached by a narrow footpath through lush tropical village gardens. Similar to the monastery, the valavva is built around a small inner courtyard though it appears even more modest than the *pansala*. The walls are constructed with mud from the paddy fields and the roof is covered with rice straw. Inside it does not differ very much from an ordinary peasant house, though a number of stools for low caste people to sit on and the ground plan of the house indicate its aristocratic connections. The family occupying this manor and an other one nearby once played a major role in Kandyan history but has fallen on bad days since the head of the family was executed by the last king of Kandy and the family lost most of its land in subsequent years. The beneficiary has largely been the Buddhist section of the Lankatilaka temple so that the former feudal village of Arawawwala is now a temple village. The present temple lord *(basnāyaka nilamē)* of the Lankatilaka Devale, about whom more will be said in the next chapter, lives in a manor of somewhat more solid construction a few miles south of Lankatilaka.

I have so far described the "physical plant" of the Lankatilaka temple complex, and I can now turn to a short description of the most permanent inhabitants around whom most of the activities revolve, namely Buddha and the seven gods. After that I want to add some remarks about the history of Lankatilaka and then turn to those who govern the temple's activities: monks, priests and landlords.

2. Buddha and the Seven Gods

The structure of the pantheon venerated at Lankatilaka is reflected in the distribution of images and shrines over the temple complex. The center is occupied by the image of the Buddha who holds the highest position in the pantheon. His personal characteristics, as well as his religious qualities, are quite different from those of the gods, godlings and demons. His concern is strictly "otherworldly". He has achieved nirvana, he has left this world and can therefore not interfere in its turbulent history directly. He has appointed some of the gods as guardian deities of Buddhist Ceylon, and all applications for the redress of grievances have therefore to be addressed to them or to those godlings and demons to whom they have in turn relegated their authority—a perfect bureaucratic system.

The basic division of religious concern and competence for betterment of this life on one hand, and a more pleasant rebirth or ultimate salvation on the other, is the basis for the dual structure of Lankatilaka's architecture, and its social, religious and economic organization.[1]

The guardian deities represented at Lankatilaka are *Viṣṇu*, the chief guardian deity, and four gods responsible for one of the cardinal directions and regions each: *Saman* (West), *Kataragama* (South), *Vibhīṣaṇa* (East) and *Gana* (North). Most of these gods have a principal temple in their respective areas, *Viṣṇu* in Kandy (Central Province), *Saman* in Mahiyangana (Province of Uva in eastern Ceylon),[2] *Kataragama* in the famous pilgrim place in the Southern Province, and *Vibhīṣaṇa* in Kälaniya (Western Province). The pattern is similar to that of Kandy where the four guardian deities are *Viṣṇu*, *Nātha*, *Kataragama* and *Pattini*, housed,however, in separate temples.

The five guardian deities occupy the shrines in the inner temple wall (see figure 7); the remaining two gods are of lower status and are consequently separated from their superiors. The devale of *Kumāra Baṇḍāra Dēviyō*, the "prince God", is added to the inner temple wall, and the temple of *Dädimuṇḍa Dēvatā Baṇḍāra Deviyō* is a separate building on the temple compound (see figure 6). *Dädimuṇḍa*, also called *Alutnuvara Deviyo*, is the commander-in-chief *(senapati)* of Visnu and heads an army on 11,500 demons *(yaksha)*.[3] He defended the Buddha when he was attacked by *Māra* before his enlightenment. All these gods play a major role in Sinhalese religion. Their mythology and their special powers are often described in Sinhalese manuscripts and in modern pamphlets based on older texts. The priests recite some of these stories in front of the gods. They know them by heart and refresh their memory by reading cheap editions available in Kandy or at the major pilgrim places. Though I have checked

1 For further discussions of this point see Obeyesekere 1966, Ames 1964, Evers 1964b, 1968a).

2 The most important Saman temple today is at Ratnapura. See Paranavitana 1958 for further details.

3 This figure was mentioned by one of the priests.

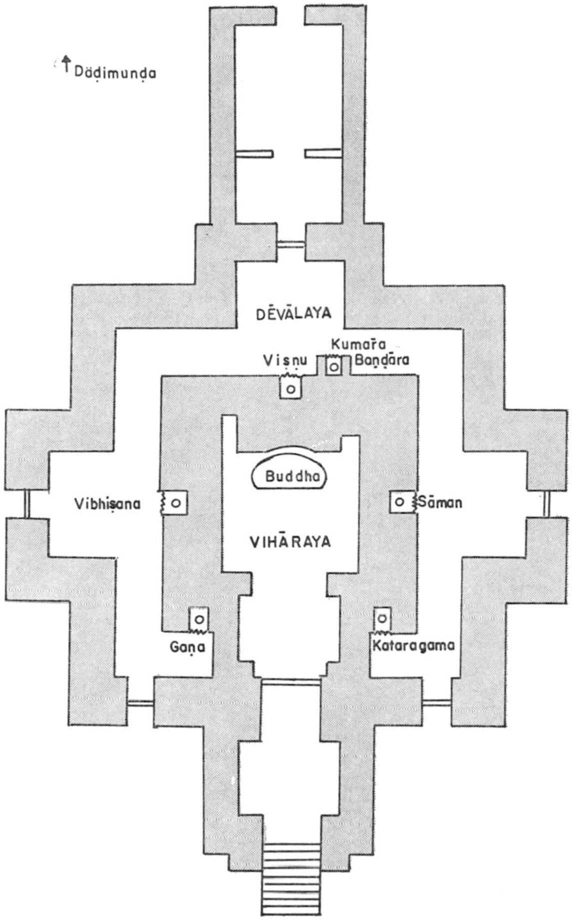

Fig. 7
Lankātilaka Temple — The vihāra with the Principal Buddha image is surrounded on three sides by the dēvāle with the images of the gods.

some of these texts I have in most cases relied on oral tradition, i.e. the stories as told by the Lankatilaka priests.

The main protector of Buddhism in Ceylon is *Upulvan (Kihiräli Upulvan* or *Varuna)*, but this god is now identified with *Viṣṇu* (Evers 1968a: 543, Paranavitana 1953). Lankatilaka Devale is now regarded as a Visnu temple and all the temple land is dedicated to this god. Though the priests are aware that Visnu is a major Hindu god they maintain that he is a disciple of the Buddha and acts under the Buddha's license.

Saman is most closely connected with the Buddhist religious system. He is a Bodhisattva, a future Buddha. Paranavitana (1957) has devoted a whole monograph to this god. He points out that Saman was originally regarded a *dēvarāja*, a king of gods, residing on Ceylon's holy mountain, the Adam's peak. (1957: 22)[1]

Gana is identical with the Indian elephant-headed Ganesha. Though he is included in the temple ritual people do not turn to him for help. The same holds true for *Vibīṣhaṇa*, a demon *(Yaksha)* who has risen to the status of a god *(deviyo)*. He is a brother of the demon king *Rāvanā* who supposedly ruled Ceylon in a mythical past and is an important figure in the classical Sanskrit epos, the *Rāmāyana*. He is more important in South India where he is believed to have founded the important temple town of Sri Rangam. Another god who has experienced a very impressive degree of upward social mobility is *Kataragama (Ṣkandha* or *Khanda Kumāra)*. Obeyesekere (1966: 25) feels "that this deity will soon become, next to the Buddha, the predominant deity in the pantheon and may eventually displace the other guardian deities altogether." God Kataragama is a son of *Śiva*, who married a vädda maiden and settled down in Southern Ceylon. His main temple at the village of Kataragama has become one of the major pilgrim centres of Ceylon (Bechert 1967, Wirtz 1954b), and his growing fame has boosted the attention given to him at other temples, including Lankatilaka.

The most powerful god at Lankatilaka is, however, *Kumāra Baṇḍāra*. Nobody, not even the priests themselves, dare to look at the small (about 2 feet high) black statue of the god hidden behind a curtain. Whoever looks at the image will either die or become blind which in fact happened to a priest in 1922 after seeing the statue. In 1928 another priest fell from a tree and died after violating the taboo. His sons dared not stay in the area and sold all their temple land to their father's brother who then became priest. But even he was not safe from the wrath of the god and lost both hands when falling from a tree. The present priest *(Kapurāḷa)* who related these frightful stories takes great care, as I could observe myself, not to look at the image during the ritual and to be ritually clean before entering the devale.

The story of Kumara Bandara is worthwhile relating as it might provide us with some insight into how a Sinhalese Buddhist perceives his gods, which in turn influences his attitudes and behavior towards the devale section of the Lankatilaka Temple complex.[2]

A son of the king of Soli had a traffic accident in which he killed a calf with his chariot. His father, a just king, had a bell in front of his palace which anybody could strike to whom injustice had been done. The cow, mother of the killed calf, made use of this arrangement, rang the bell and made her complaints known to the king, who became very angry and decided that justice should be done. To punish his son he decreed that he also should be run

---

1 In another publication Paranavitana (1959: 524, France-Asie 153–157) identifies Saman with "Samantabhadra, one of the eight principal Mahayanist Bodhisattvas." Both this point as well as the fact that Saman resides on a mountain as god-king *(dēvarāja)*, invites an explanation related to Southeast Asian history.

2 For other versions of the following story see Mss. nrs. 742, 796 in the Neville collection of Sinhalese kavi manuscripts, catalogued in Deraniyagala 1954–55, and Barnett 1917.

over by a chariot. Very cunningly, however, he had a pit dug in the ground and his son placed into it. One of his ministers was then asked to drive across the pit in his chariot. Unfortunately the prince was too curious of what was going on. He stuck his head out of the pit and it was instantaneously chopped off by the approaching chariot. To console the queen, who was desperate at the death of her son, the king had an image of the prince made. The image was placed in the palace, but whatever direction it faced great disasters would happen in that part of the country. The statue was then taken away by ship and thrown into the Indian Ocean. Shortly thereafter the image appeared at Ceylon's northern coast and was brought to Ridi Vihara in Central Ceylon. But as disasters happened here too, the image was transferred to Lankatilaka in about 1840 and placed back to back to the pricipal Buddha image, which apparently neutralized some of its powers.[1] After a special offering in the new god's honour lost cattle were suddenly found. People then started to believe in the god's power and he has drawn large crowds of worshippers ever since.

The story of the genesis of this god gains more significance when we compare it with similar stories in other Theravada Buddhist countries. Both the town spirits venerated in Thailand and some important nats in Burma (Spiro 1967: 41) originated from persons who died a violent death at the hand of others. Though this similarity does not necessarily prove any direct cultural influence, it does show certain parallel features in the religious structure of Theravada Buddhism which are often overlooked.

The other Bandara god, *Dädimuṇḍa Dēvatā Baṇḍāra*, has an equally interesting story. He also seems to have gained in importance during the last three centuries when many small separate devales were built on the compounds of Visnu temples to satisfy the demands of pious customers. As his main temple is not at Lankatilaka but at Alutnuvara, Kegalle District, I shall pass over his history.[2]

As I have indicated in this chapter the relations between the Buddha and the gods, and among the gods themselves, have changed. A brief look at the history of Lankatilaka will provide us with an example of the development of Sinhalese religion.

3. The History of Lankatilaka

A stone inscription next to the temple fixes the date of its construction as 1344 A.C. The first half of the 14th century was a period of rapid change in South and Southeast Asia. Most of the Dekhan and South India had come under Muslim rule which in turn provoked the resurgence of a fanatic Saivism. "In its single-minded devotion to Siva, its fanatical intolerance of the followers

1 According to another informant the image was already at Lankatilaka during Portuguese times when a temple official rescued it from Portuguese destructive and religious fervour during a raid on the temple. Considering the risk involved in dealing with this god I did not examine the shrine or the image closer to clarify the matter.

2 See Nevill's collection of Kavi mss. nrs. 36, 182, 267, 303, 601–4. Deraniyagala 1954–55.

of any other creed, whom it stigmatized as *bhavis* (infidels), and in its ideal of perfect equality among the *bhaktas*, the new Saivism was a worthy rival of Islam..." (Sastri 1958: 227). The Sinhalese Buddhists of Ceylon were thus isolated on the farthest tip of South Asia and threatened by two expansionist religious movements. Perhaps only the rise of Vijayanagar, the last of the great Hindu empires, saved Ceylon from Islamization. Relations with Southeast Asia however, where Buddhism flourished continued to be strong. Frequent visits by Sinhalese monks in Thailand and Burma are recorded in texts and inscriptions. (Paranavitana in Ray 1960: 754–56).

Theravada Buddhism was by then firmly established in mainland Southeast Asia, not, however, as the religion of wandering ascetics but as the state religion of the Southeast Asian god-kings. If we regard all Theravada Buddhist countries of that time as one cultural area with the same major religion it is warranted to assume that other connected patterns of beliefs, social structure and political organization showed traces of common characteristics.[1] On the other hand, South Indian influences must have been quite strong in Ceylon through immigration of mercenaries, aristocrats, and Brahmins fleeing the Muslim expansion.

Ceylon itself was torn by strife and divided into at least three different kingdoms during this time. Parakramabahu V (1344–1350) ruled the Western lowlands from the capital of Dädigama and Bhuvanaikabahu IV (1341–1351) in whose reign and demand the Lankatilaka temple was built, ruled Central Ceylon from his capital of Gampola. Both were harassed by the Tamil-Hinduist king of Jaffna in Northern Ceylon, the Ariya Cakravartin, who invaded and subdued the realms of the Sinhalese Buddhist kings several times, probably with the help of South Indian armies. (Paranavitana in Ray 1960: 636–652). This period was further characterized by the struggle between two powerful warrior-ministers and their families: Sena Lankadhikara, the builder of Lankatilaka temple, and Alagakkonara (or Alakesvara) of Rayigama in Southwestern Ceylon. It appears that Sinhalese rulers had to face two major political problems which were directly related to the foundation of Lankatilaka temple: (1) the conflict over who would be recognized as the sovereign of Sri Lanka and the Sinhalese and (2) the fight against the Northern invasions which had plagued the Sinhalese for centuries and was to last until the arrival of the European maritime powers in the 16th century.

The first problem was not only a matter of intrigue, war and regicide, but of legitimacy. Both Sena Lankadhikara and Alagakkonara were aspirants to the thron. They both furthered the creation of fictional genealogies linking them with Indian royalty (Rajaratnakara, cited by Paranavitana 1960: 640).

---

1 Paranavitana (1966) has in a recent monograph analysed the close contacts between Ceylon and Southeast Asia, mainly Nakhorn Sri Thammarat in Southern Thailand, Sumatra and Java. The rather unfortunate compartmentalization into South and Southeast Asian studies and the dominance of the India centric view have probably tended to obscure Southeast Asian influences on Ceylon and India. Paranavitana's theory has, however, not remained unchallenged. See Indrapala 1967.

The possession of royal insignia[1], the performance of royal ritual by Brahmins and the building of royal temples for the Sinhalese guardian deities became of great importance in this connection. To retain the allegiance of the Buddhist Sinhalese population and the Buddhist monkhood against the Hindu invaders, donations of land and construction of Buddhist shrines and monasteries might have been seen as essential for the solution of the second problem.

Sena Lankadhikara was therefore actively supporting the Buddhist monkhood. In 1341 he convened an assembly of Buddhist monks, conducted an inquisition, and had those monks expelled from the order who did not live according to the vinaya rules. He also constructed a number of Buddhist temples, including the Lankatilaka temple and a shrine in Conjeevaram in South India (Nicholas and Paranavitana 1961: 330). It could well be that the construction of temples and the donation of land and slaves was a deliberate political move by Sena Lankadhikara to win the allegiance of the Buddhist monkhood and to consolidate his own power by landholdings which were safe from confiscation by the king. The Lankatilaka stone inscription of 1344 states expressly that Sena Lankadhikara and his lineal descendents should be in charge of the temple, whereas the king just confirms the land grant. The Mahanavara family headed by Sena would thus control the temple lands and temple serfs because the king could not alienate what had been given to the Buddha and the Gods. It seems that this policy was followed by other Sinhalese feudal lords up to the end of the Sinhalese empire in 1815.

From the Lankatilaka inscription it is clear that Sena Lankadhikara and his family were the prime donors of the temple and were responsible for its construction around 1344. It is not clear whether the temple was fully completed in 1344, but at least in the reign of Parakramabahu VI (1412–1467) after some repairs had been made (Mahavamsa 91: 30) it had reached its final unique form. For the first time in Ceylonese history the fusion of Buddhism and the cult of gods found its spatial and architectural expression in one temple. "As late as the twelfth century there is no evidence that the gods had any special place of worship provided for them *inside* Buddhist monasteries. The destination of the various buildings attached to Buddhist monasteries is not always known; yet if we take an important group of Buddhist shrines, such as the Quadrangle at Polonnaruva, we can say with certainty that it did not include any temple of the gods, though the very close proximity of a Siva temple in Pandyan style, that is 13th century, seems to foreshadow the Hindu invasion of the Buddhist monastery." (Hocart 1926: 19). An important question in the social and religious history of Ceylon is thus posed by the architecture and the distribution of "religious space" in Lankatilaka: Why did the interrelation between Buddhism and the cult of gods reach its climax in the 14th century, at least in temple building? Pointing to the South Indian influences and the influx of Brahmins does not provide sufficient evidence. South Indian

1 According to Arab traveller Ibn Batuta, who visited Ceylon in 1344, Alagakonara was in the possession of a white elephant.

influences alone could have led, as during most of the Polonnaruva period, to the construction of *separate* Hindu temples. We could also have expected the division of the Sinhalese into different religious sects. Neither of the things happened. A sociological explanation will be attempted in chapter VI of this study. To find a historical explanation we may have to take South Indian as well as Southeast Asian cultural contacts into consideration. The fusion of Buddhism and Hinduism was still flourishing in Indonesia at that time and the cult of the godking was carried on in a Buddhist framework in Thailand and Burma in a more pronounced form than in Ceylon before. Another attempt at explanation would be to take Lankatilaka as a cultural symbol expressing the anxiety of Sinhalese leaders in a time of decline. The guardian deities of Ceylon form a protective ring around the Buddha who is here seen as the cultural symbol of the Sinhalese race. Vibhisana, who has already helped the Buddha in fight against Mara before he attained nirvana, as well as the warrior god Skanda (Kataragama), are employed to defend Buddha, Dhamma and Sangha and those who take refuge in them.

During the Gampola period Lankatilaka and its sister temples at Gadaladeniya and Ämbäkka must have played an important role which was somewhat diminished when the court moved to Kandy and the four Kandy devales, together with the Temple of the Tooth Relic *(Daḷadā Māḷigāva)*, came into prominence. It is, however, safe to assume that Lankatilaka has functioned with only minor interruptions during foreign invasions for more than 600 years.[1]

1 As only a few notes on the history of Lankatilaka could be supplied, a list of major sources is added.

Cave, H. W., 1908, The Book of Ceylon, London: Cassell & Co.; pp. 242, 337–339.

Codrington, H. W., 1936, A Short History of Ceylon, London: MacMillan, pp. 83, 86, 88, 185–186.

——, 1928–33, "Gavuta Pillars", Ceylon Journal of Science, Sect. G, II, p. 133.

Evers, Hans-Dieter, 1968, "Buddha and the Seven Gods, the Dual Structure of a Temple in Central Ceylon", Journal of Asian Studies, 27: 541–550.

Gunasekara, B., 1887, "Three Sinhalese Inscriptions: Text, Transliteration, Translation and Notes," Journal Ceylon Branch Royal Asiatic Society X, No. 34, pp. 83–105.

Hocart, A. M., 1926, "The Kandyan Lankatilaka", Archaeological Survey of Ceylon, Vol. 2, Colombo: Government Printer, pp. 18–21.

Lankātilaka Sannas Liyavilla, n.d., (Sinhalese ms), Neville Mss. Nr. 52 British Museum Library, Oriental Manuscripts Collection.

Mudiyanse, N., 1965, The Art and Architecture of the Gampola Period (1341–1415 A.D.), Colombo: M. D. Sunasena.

Mahavamsa, Th. Geiger, trl., 91: 30.

Muller, Ancient Inscriptions of Ceylon, Colombo: No. 167, No. 171.

Nampota, n.d., (Sinhalese ms.), British Museum, Oriental Manuscript Collection, Wickramasinghe Catalogue 31, III Fol. 11-12b. (also several printed editions in Ceylon).

Paranavitana, S., 1960, "Lankatilaka Inscriptions", University of Ceylon Review XVIII, pp. 1–45.

——, 1928–33, "Epigraphical Summary", Ceylon Journal of Science, Sect. G, II, pp. 188, 213.

——, 1960, "Lankatilaka", in University of Ceylon, History of Ceylon, Vol. I, Part II, Colombo: Ceylon University Press, pp. 782–785.

CHAPTER THREE

Social Organization: Secular and Religious Temple Administration

1. The Temple Officials

THE present social organization of Lankatilaka is a remnant of Kandyan feudal structure, modified and changed by colonial legislation and modern trends in Sinhalese society. The basic features have, however, remained intact.

In accordance with the religious differentiation into a vihara and a devale, the social organization is also bifurcated. Both the vihara and the devale system follow, however, a similar organizational pattern. There are three organizational levels in both systems: secular officials, religious specialists and their attendants, and temple tenants. (Table 6).

Conflicts between the levels are frequent and in the case of other temples have lead to extensive court cases. Especially in the Kandy Kataragama devale,

Table 6

Administrative Structure of Lankatilaka Temple

Vihara	*Dēvāle*	*Main function*
I Vihārādhipati	Basnāyaka Nilamē	Trustee, Landlord
Vidāna	Vidāna	Temple headman
Pannikalayā	Vaṇṇakurāla	Overseer over III
II Bhikkhu	Kapurāla	"Priest"
Multänrāla	Multänrāla	Cook of offerings
Vatarāla (= Vaterurāla)	Vatarāla (= Vaterurāla)	Attendant at rituals
III Nilakārayā	Nilakārayā	Temple servant
(a) Attendants at daily offerings	(a) Attendants at bi-weekly offerings	e.g. Musicians, dancers (dēvāle only)
(b) Supplier of food, flowers, etc. for offerings	(b) Supplier of food, etc. for offerings	
(c) Attendants at festivals	(c) Attendants at festivals	
(d) Workers of rice fields, repairs, cleaning, etc.	(d) Workers of rice fields, repairs, cleaning, etc.	

where the priests are prestigious Tamil Brahmins, the authority of the secular temple officials is often challenged.

The heads of the temple administration are the viharadhipati and the basnayaka nilame. The viharadhipati or chief incumbent of Lankatilaka Vihara was, until his death in 1968, Amunugama Rajaguru Siri Vipassi Mahanayaka Thero. He was born in 1907 as a member of the Kandyan Aristocracy *(radala)* in Yatinuvara, Kandy District. In his early boyhood he was ordained into the Buddhist order as pupil of the Mahanayaka of Malvatta, Amunugama Rajaguru Siri Nivasa Piyadassi, who was also chief incumbent of Lankatilaka and of another important temple, Kobbäkaduva Raja Maha Vihara at Murutalava, Yatinuvara. Siri Vipassi was educated at the Vidyodaya Pirivena in Kelaniya and received his higher ordination *(upasampadā)* at Malvatta in 1929. Some years before the ordination, in 1924, his teacher Siri Nivasa had died and he had succeeded him as viharadhipati of Lankatilaka. As he was then only 17 years old and still a *sāmaṇera* (novice), a caretaker was appointed until he could take over the office as head of the temple in 1929 according to ecclesiastical law. In 1951 he was elected Anunayaka and in 1964 Mahanayaka of Malwatta. He had then achieved what is considered to be the highest position in the Sinhalese Sangha, the chief monk of the largest and oldest nikaya.

Sri Vipassi had succeeded to the office of viharadhipati according to a traditional rule of succession, the *śiṣyānuśiṣya paramparāva*. This rule decrees that the first ordained pupil of a viharadhipati will succeed him and inherit his temple property.[1]

The office of viharadhipati is therefore inherited, though not on a kinship basis. The line of succession is established by an ordination lineage, the *paramparāva*, in which the most senior pupil inherits office and property according to a principle similar to that of primogeniture in kinship systems. In addition to the religious relationship (between monk-teachers and pupils or between successive viharadhipatis), kinship relations have, however, also played a major part. At least the past five viharadhipatis have been closely related. All of them were radala, that is members of the relatively small aristocratic subcaste of the highest Sinhalese caste, which in itself makes kinship relations plausible. Siri Vipassi's senior pupil, who will succeed him, is again a close relative, namely his mother's younger brother's son *(massina)*. (Table 7).

The *basnāyaka nilamē* is also a radala. "Kirinda Nilame", as he is called by the villagers, lives in his manor *(valavva)* not far from the old town of Gampola. He visits Lankatilaka only occasionally because he is rather busy administering his own private temple he has built on the second floor of his house. The temple is dedicated to Visnu and the nine planetary deities. Worshippers are assured in a printed prospectus that a charm obtained and donned in front of the principal image is beneficial:

1 This rule is further discussed in SP XVIII, 1959, Buddha Sāsana Komiśan Vartāva, 137–149, in Bechert 1966: 225–226, and Evers 1967a. Information given in Ryan 1953: 41, Wood 1961: 14 and Bareau 1957: 72–74 is not correct.

Table 7
Temple Chiefs of Lankātilaka

Vihārādhipatis	
1890–1924	Amunugama Rajaguru Siri Nivasa Piyadassi Mahanayaka Thero (1919–1924)
1924–1968	Amunugama Rajaguru Siri Vipassi Mahanayaka Thero (1964–1968)
	Trustees: Rambukvälle Siri Siddhattha (Temporary, 1924–?) and Minuvangamuve Siri Sumana (Nayaka Thero of Udunuvara)
1968–	Amunugama Siri Piyadasi
Basnāyaka Nilamēs	
1918–1949	U.B. Walgampaya of Embilimigama
1949–1959	P. B. Kapuliyada of Bowala
1959–1969	H. W. Kirinda of Galgediyawa

"1. For good health, cures diseases.
2. For wealth and happiness.
3. Success in profession-whatever it may be.
4. Success in love of man and love of woman.
5. Success in Examination.
6. To overcome enemies, opponents, rivals and competitors.
7. Blessings of children to barren women, and to those whose children don't live long.
8. To conquer and overcome enemies, black magic and psychic forces.
9. To conquer evil influences of planets and Spirits."

Kirinde Nilame claims that he has inherited a golden palm-leaf manuscript from one of his forefathers who was the Keeper of the King's Granary at the court of Bhuvanayaka Bahu VI of Gampola. Some time ago he decided to extend the benefits of the thus related "mystical science ...based upon the Sacred Holy powers of Maha Sri Vishnu, the Guardian God of Lanka (Ceylon)" to the welfare of his country and his customers—against payment of an appropriate honorarium.

The office of basnayaka nilame in not hereditary. H. W. Kirinda was elected chief of Lankatilaka devale in 1959 by a special electorate as prescribed in the Buddhist Temporalities Ordinance of 1931. This electorate consists of the divisional revenus officers (D.R.O.) of the Kandy District, the Diyawandana Nilame of the Dalada Maligave, the basnayaka nilames of all devales in the Kandy District and the trustees of all viharas situated in Udunuvara and Yatinuvara as far as they are not Buddhist monks (section 8.2 of the Ordinance). There were all together 76 voters at his election. After being elected basnayaka he is also appointed trustee of Lankatilaka devale by the Public Trustee in Colombo, who presides during the election proceedings. The appointment is for a ten year term.

Siri Vipassi is also appointed trustee of Lankatilaka vihara by the Public Trustee. He is, however, not elected but has made use of provision 10 of the Buddhist Temporalities Ordinance, which gives the viharadhipati the right to nominate the trustee. He has subsequently nominated himself.

The major function of both the viharadhipati and the basnayaka is the administration of the extensive temple lands and the organization of the temple festivals. They are therefore primarily aristocratic landlords in a system which Max Weber has termed "monastic landlordism" (Weber 1958: 257).

The viharadhipati hardly ever officiates at religious rituals at the vihara. Only on special occasions (e.g. during one of the four annual temple festivals), will he be present and take part in the ritual. Nevertheless he used to drive out to Lanaktilaka in his car approximately once a week or a fortnight to attend to matters of temple administration. His role as temple landlord is perhaps most significantly enacted during the annual ceremony of allegiance of temple tenants, and I shall therefore give a brief description of the event.

On January 2nd, 1966, the day of the "New Rice Festival" *(alut sal mangalaya)*, the viharadhipati, Sri Vipassi Mahanayaka Thero, his senior pupil Piyadassi Thero, and three other bhikkus normally residing at Lankatilaka, had assembled for their noon meal in the refectory *(dansalāva)* of the monastery *(pansala)*. Rice and a fair number of curries had been prepared by the three temple boys from supplies out of the vihara storehouse, the vihara garden and others items bought at the local boutique (village shop). Nevertheless the meal is still called *dāna*, "a charitable gift to bhikkus" in accordance with the ideology that the sangha should be supported by laymen who earn religious merit *(pin)* through gifts to bkikhhus. Danas arranged by villagers are, however, celebrated on other occasions. (See chapter IV).

After the meal the Mahanayaka and his disciple proceed to the small porch in the inner courtyard where the venerable Sri Vipassi settles down on a couch and Piyadassi Thero on an armchair. The sociologist is offered a small chair somewhat lower than both the couch and the armchair.

In the meantime the temple tenants and their headmen have assembled in front of the pansala. They now enter through the main door and line up in the inner courtyard, the tenants from the village of Rabbegamuwa on one side, those from Arawwawala and Godawela on the other. They then proceed one after the other to the porch, kneel before the Mahanayaka and his disciple, hand over some betel leaves to one of them, and touch the floor with their foreheads three times. While they still kneel Vipassi Thero checks their names in a little booklet of the type purchased by school children for their homework with a portrait of Queen Elizabeth and Prince Philip on the blue cover. The betel leaves *(bulat)* are traditional symbols of allegiance and respect and are widely used in Sinhalese ritual. The act of paying homage to the landlord and presenting him with betel leaves, called a *penuma*, is understood as the reconfirmation of a landlord—tenant relationship and was widely practised in Kandyan times (Pieris 1956: 68, 117).

Then the headmen of the tenants come forward and offer excuses for those tenants who did not turn up because of illness or family obligations. The Mahanayaka admonishes the tenants to do their temple services properly. He takes some of the betel leaves piled up on a table and hands them back to the headmen. They first exchange some betel leaves among themselves and then redistribute the rest among their tenants, who leave the pansala after some further discussion.

The headmen or overseers of temple tenants of the temple villages have, for reasons I could not clearly establish, different titles. The overseer from Rabbegamuva is called *vidāna*. A vidana was in Kandyan times a village representative of a provincial governor *(disāva)* (Pieris 1956: 25), but the term was later applied to different types of headmen. The overseer from Arawwawala is referred to as *panikkayā* (chief of tom-tom beater's caste) or sometimes as *panikkalē*, a title originally reserved for officers of the *kūruva* or the Department of Elephants in the Kandyan kingdom. The overseer from Godewela is called *durayā*, originally a headman of a low caste, (Pieris 1956: 292). This title is also known in devale administration and is mentioned in a list of devale officers of the Sabaragamuva Province, compiled by Herbert Wright in 1818, (Reprinted in Pieris 1956: 33–36), and of officers in a village of the Dalada Maligava (Pieris 1956: 77).

The rank order of the headmen implied in their titles vidana, panikkale and duraya, is connected with the caste status of the villagers they are in charge of. This will be further discussed in a later chapter. On the whole, the power of the viharagam headmen is rather restricted and their major function is to transmit the viharadhipati's orders to his tenants. Their office is not hereditary, and the chief monk is free to appoint whomever he sees fit. In fact the office of vidana and panikkale has been held by members of different families. The overseers, however, always resided in the respective temple village.

The present vidana of the devale tenants, G. G. Mudiyanse of Tirappuva, is a much more powerful figure. He is also appointed by the temple landlord, but the basnayaka nilame, in contrast to the viharadhipati, hardly ever visits the temple or the temple villages, except during the annual perahära or another important occasion, like the staging of a special temple festival for an European film company in 1965. This gives the vidana autonomy in handling day to day devale affairs. The vidana is himself a big landowner by village standards and his prestigious vasagama name indicates that he regards himself a member of the former Goyigama "bureaucratic elite" of the Kandyan Kingdom. He keeps the keys of the devale, oversees the services of temple tenants and is in charge of the cash box into which the offerings of devotees are placed. His power is considerably strenghtened by the fact that he knows the necessary chants to address the gods in the devale himself and can therefore also act as priest. He also claims the right to impose fines of up to five Rupees on tenants for failing to perform their duty *(rājakāriya)*, though I have not heard of recent cases where he has actually done so.

The vidana's assistant is the vannakurala who also happens to be the priest *(kapurāḷa)* of the Dädimunda Devata (or Alutnuvara) Devale. He is present at the weekly rituals, looks daily after the devale, acts as messenger to inform the temple musicians when the next ritual is going to take place and arranges the minor temple festivals. He lives at the end of the procession street, where his son runs a small village tea house. *Vannaku* means literally accounts.

The viharadhipati and the basnayaka nilame, with their respective assistants, form the temple administration. The next group to be discussed are the religious functionaries.

2. Religious Specialists: Monks and Priests

As was mentioned earlier, the viharadhipati usually stays at the Malvatta monastery in Kandy and does not perform the daily rituals at Lankatilaka. This is done by a bhikkhu, the venerable Buddharakhita Thero, whom the Mahanayaka appointed in 1956. He receives board and lodging and a monthly salary of about Rs. 50.– for his duty. Buddharakhita is, as all monks of the Siyam Nikaya, of Goyigama caste origin, and was born in a nearby village. He is not a member of the Mahanayaka's ordination lineage *(paramparāva)*, but the disciple of a vihardhipati of a small vihara at Embekke, about 1½ miles from Lankatilaka as the crow flies. When his teacher dies he plans to return to his home village and take over his temple.

There are two other monks staying at Lankatilaka pansala. One is a teacher in a village school near Galagedara, about ten miles from Kandy, and visits Lankatilaka only on weekends or during the school holidays. The other is a novice *(sāmaṇera)* from an ancient, but isolated temple in the North Central Province not far from the classical centre of Sinhalese culture and Buddhism, Anuradhapura. He visits the Sangharaja Pirivena, a monk's college at Kandy, where the Mahanayaka is principal. He is under the authority of Buddharakhita Thero, who asks him to do small jobs around the pansala and also teases him frequently about his native village in the *vanni*, a supposedly uncultured and underdeveloped jungle area. The samanera Ananda also performs a small ritual every morning, the *mal pūjāva*, on his own and joins Buddharakhita in reciting *gathas* (Pali verses) in the vihara.

Buddharakhita's counterpart in the devale is the *kapurāḷa*. As we will see in the next chapter both their ritual functions are very similar. Their social role is, however, different. In fact, it is not only different but the decisive role elements are opposed binary categories. The bhikkhu has to observe celibacy, the kapurala has to be married; the bhikkhu has to shave his head, the kapurala is expected to have long hair (note the sexual or fertility connotation of long hair!); the monk takes part in funeral rites, the priest is polluted by death and consequently shuns funerals and funeral houses; the Buddhist monk is dressed in a ceremonial garment, the saffran colored robe; the priest of the gods dresses as any other villager except during rituals, when he either wears an elaborate and colorful uniform or at least covers his head with a scarf.

The *kapu mahatmaya (kapurāḷa)* is also endowed with special faculties and power. He knows verses *(kavi)* which, if chanted before a god, might either harm or benefit a person (*vaskavi* and *setikavi* respectively). His power is necessary to survive the dangers encountered in dealing with the gods whose power is considerably greater. Two former kapuralas of Lankatilaka are said to have died because of a slight mistake in the performance of ritual. One fell from a coconut tree and broke his neck, the other was bitten by a snake and was poisoned. The present kapuralas claim some knowledge of anti-snakebite poisons and charms, though they are supposedly not in danger of being stung as long as they perform their ritual properly and keep ritually pure. They are therefore not endangered by the cobras, living in the devale itself. (This is no fabrication. I was at first skeptical about the claim that snakes are found in the devale until I actually observed some creeping in and out of the shrines.)

There are three kapuralas at Lankatilaka. One of them performs the weekly rituals, the other officiates during the main festival. The third kapurala is the already-mentioned vanakkurala, who is in charge of the small separate Dädimunda Devata Devale.

Bulumulla Mudiyanselegedera Hinbanda, the *dolosmase kapurāḷa* (12-months kapurala) lives at Hiddaulla. He traces his origin back to a Brahmin caste *(bamuṇu kula)* settled at the village of Bulumulla in Yatinuvara, about three miles north of Lankatilaka.[1] King Bhuvanaika Bahu VI appointed a member of that caste as kapurala after Lankatilaka was built in 1344 A.C. From that time the office was apparently handed down patrilineally to the present incumbent of the position. Claims of Brahmin origin are occasionally made by members of Sinhalese caste who want to upgrade the status of their whole caste (e.g. among the Navandanna or smiths; Ryan 1953: 113). The Niti Nighanduva, an 18th or early -19th century text, argues that the high status of the Goyigama caste is due to frequent intermarriages with Brahmins from India. Individuals are, however, not known to assert descendance from a distinct Brahmin caste in the existing literature nor is there such a caste in present day Sinhalese society.

Despite the fact that Hinbanda placed great emphasis on his patrilineal predecessors and on the unbroken succession of kapuralas, he could not trace his ancestry further back than three generations. Some data on his kinship relations might serve to indicate the intellectual climate and social network in which a kapurala operates. (See figure 8).

Hinbanda's grandfather (A: 1) was born in the 1840's at Hiyarapitiya. He inherited about five päl (2¼ acres) of temple land from his father and took over his office of kapurala, which he later passed on to one of his sons (B: 1), Hin-

1 Bechert (1968a: 290) claims that a large number of Brahmin families migrated to Sinhalese areas during the 14th and 15th centuries. These families, including those which still serve the temples given to their ancestors, have merged with the Goyigama castes. Bechert's claim is substantiated by the family tradition of the Lankatilaka priest. In the Niti-Nighanduva the migration of Brahmins to Ceylon is described as follows (p. 6): "Representatives of the Raja Bamunu (Brahmin) and Velanda castes had from time to time come over to live here. They did not, however, preserve their castes intact, but intermarried with the goviya caste, and it is for this reason, that the goviya is considered the chief caste in this kingdom."

banda's father. Another son (B: 2) became a Buddhist monk and received his higher ordination as one of the pupils of Amunugama Siri Nivasa Mahanayaka Thero, the then viharadhipati of Lankatilaka Vihara. He later lived at a pansala at Hendeniya (Gangapalata, Undunuvara). Another son (B: 3) died young and unmarried, and three daughters (B: 4, 5, 6) married in Hiyarapitiya.

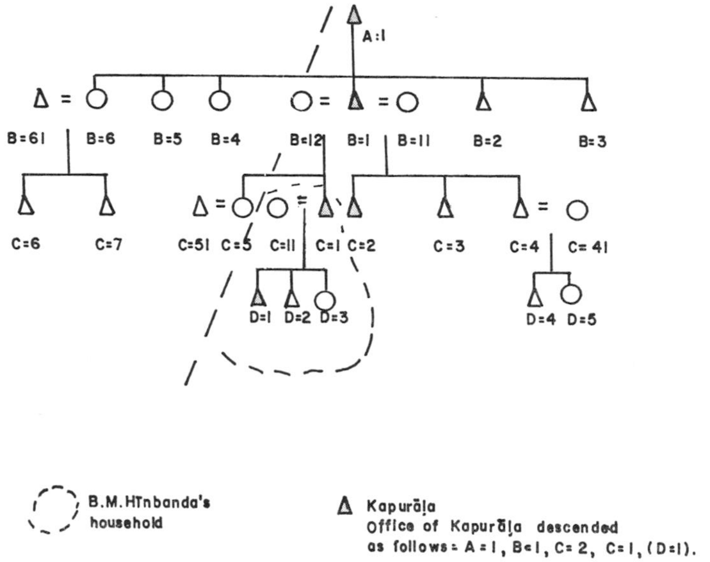

Fig. 8
Genealogy of a Lankatilaka Kapurāla

Our Kapurala's father was born in 1868 or 1869 at Hiyarapitiya, but later moved to Hidaulla. During his long life he had four sons (C: 1, 2, 3, 4) and one daughter (: 5) from two wives (B: 11, 12). One wife was from Pata Hewaheta, the other from Yatinuvara. Hinbanda's eldest brother (C: 2, born 1895) helped his father as kapurala, after he was married to a wife from Nawalapitiya, some 15 miles from Lankatilaka. He later took over the office himself, until he suddenly sold his inherited share of temple land to an outsider, left the village and settled on newly opened land at the Galoya irrigation scheme in the Eastern Province. He usually comes to Lankatilaka during the perahära seasons and acts as kapurala for a week.

The next brother (C: 3, born 1917) was robed as Buddhist monk, received his higher ordination at Asgiriya vihara, Kandy, and lived in a temple near Teldeniya (Pata Dumbara). He later disrobed himself, married and settled at the Kantalai Colonization scheme near Tincomalee. The third brother (C: 4, born 1923) is now a labourer with the Irrigation Department at Anuradhapura. He still has a stake in his former village community through ownership of one-half acre of temple land. This paddy land is worked by Hinbanda who keeps the whole harvest to himself, but he acknowledges his brother's rights by offering him a token payment or share of the produce whenever he comes to the village, which happens perhaps once in two years.

Hinbanda himself lives with his wife (who was born at Gadaladeniya, site of another famous temple), his three children and his wife's sister in a small house in the temple village of Hiddaulla, only a few minutes walk from Lankatilaka. His house has mud walls , a thatched roof and a floor hardened with a mixture of cowdung and clay. It is kept extremely tidy and clean but is otherwise no different from the houses of other poor peasants in the village. The brick houses of some of the richer villagers are small palaces in comparison. Except for the few hours in which he performs the ritual at the devala each week he spends his time as a farmer working on his own paddy fields, the fields of his brothers and on some land he has rented from a landlord. (Land tenure and related questions will be discussed in chapter V). He thus is not much distinguished from any other peasant in the village though his high caste status as Goyigama in a predominantly low caste village and his superior knowledge of traditional lore induces most other villagers to treat him with some respect. He is therefore usually referred to and addressed as *kapu mahatmaya*, a term which implies recognition of a higher status.

No formal training is required to become a kapurala. The necessary knowledge of procedure and chants is acquired through constant participation in the father's religious activities. Some of the chants used by kapuralas are available in popular prints, and the Lankatilaka kapuralas owned several of them. (For annotations to a collection of palm leaf manuscripts with chants see Deraniyagala 1954). Initiation into the office is, however, formalized. When a kapurala's son has married and it is agreed that he shall succeed his father, an auspicious date is fixed for the ensuing ceremony, usually during the perahära season.

An invitation is sent to the Basnayaka Nilame and the temple tenants informing them of the date. When all have assembled outside the devale the kapurala candidate offers betel leaves to the basnayaka and the temple tenants. Acceptance of the betel leaves signifies the approval of the participants of the new appointment. The old and the new kapurala then enter the temple and the new priest gives offerings *(pūjāva)* to the six gods. Both ask for the gods' blessings.

Of all the other persons engaged in religious activities at Lankatilaka there are two for the devale and two for the vihara whose presence is essential. These are the cook of the offerings *(multänrāḷa)* and the ritual attendant (*vatarāḷa* or *vatterurāḷa)*.[1] They are of Goyigama caste and enjoy the privilege of being allowed to enter the shrines during the ritual. The Sinhalese word

1 This office is apparently identical with that of *vattakāraka*, mentioned in the Mahavamsa 98: 27. Geiger (1960: 194) assumes that the guardians of sanctuaries *(ārakkhaka)* who were appointed by the kings since approximately the 6th century A.C., were the predecessors of the *vattakāraka*. See Mhv. 42: 21, 42: 61, 44: 69 and 44: 16.

multän (or *mulutän*) is an exalted term for food and is used only for food offered to the gods or to the Buddha. *Vata* means ritual or ceremony. Their ritual functions and their tenure of temple land will be discussed in the two following chapters.

If we compare the temple officials and religious specialists at Lankatilaka with those at other temples we find that the basic structure remains the same but that with growing size the number of officials is greater and the administrative and religious functions are more specialised. (see table 8).

Table 8

Temple Officials and Religious Specialists of the Daḷadā Māḷigāva, Kandy

Temple Officials	*Function*
Diyavaḍana Nilamē	Chief temple administrator
Kariyakorāla	Overseer, temple manager
Valavvēmohottala	Secretary of diyavadanna n.
Gabadavēmohottala	Secretary of the kariyakotala
Uḍumalēmohottala	Secretary of the upper floor
Gebarāla	Storekeeper
Pallemarāla	Storekeeper of the lower floor
Kattirāla (two)	Pingo bearers
Piun	Messenger
Hamudavalē aracci	Chief of watchmen
Religious Specialists	*Function*
Bhikkhu (two)	Ritual at upper floor shrine
Bhikkhu	Ritual at lower floor shrine
Vatterurāla	Keeper of keys and assistant at ritual
Händun kapurālas (two)	Preparation of sandalwood paste
Ālattiammā (two)	Women waving lights or incense
Multänrāla	Cook of offerings
(See Hocart 1931)	

There are also indications that the administrative structure of viharas and devales has lost some of its complexity since Kandyan times. We have already mentioned two instances at Lankatilaka: the office of vidana of the devale has merged with that of gebanarala (storekeeper) and the kapurala of the Dädimunda devale is at the same time vannakurala of the main devale.

3. Temple Tenants

The temple personnel discussed so far are grouped together as officers of inner services *(ätulkaṭṭalē rājakaranāyā)*. They are allowed to enter the shrines and are members of the highest caste, the goyigama. The other temple servants perform the outer services *(piṭakaṭṭalē)*. They can be roughly divided into groups according to the type of temple land they are holding (See Chapter V,

3). How this again is connected with the caste system and notions of ritual purity and pollution will be discussed in due course.

Most of the tenants live in three temple villages grouped around Lankatilaka, devale tenants in Hiddaulla and vihara tenants in Arawwawala and Rabbegamuwa. (See Table 9). The temple itself is situated in the village of Hiyarapitiya where only a few houses of temple tenants are to be found. With the exception of Godawela which lies on the bank of the Mahaweli River (*Maha Väli Ganga*, "Great Sand River") in Pata Hewaheta, all other villages with temple tenants and temple land are in Udunuwara. (See figure 5). Only a

Table 9
Villages of Temple Tenants

	Vihāra Tenants	*Devale Tenants*
Major temple villages	Arawwawala *(Äravvavala)*	Hiddaulla *(Hiddavulla)*
	Rabbegamuwa *(Rabbegamuva)*	
Other villages where temple tenants live	Hiyarapitiya *(Hiyarapitiya)*	Hiyarapitiya *(Hiyarapitiya)*
	Tirapuwa *(Tirappuva)*	Tirapuwa *(Tirappuva)*
	Daulagala *(Davulagala)*	
	Pamunuwa *(Pamunuva)*	Rabbegamuwa *(Rabbegamuva)*
	Godawela *(Goḍavela)*	

fraction of those who hold temple lands actually perform temple services. We must therefore distinguish between temple tenants at large and active temple servants, who do *rājakāriya* (lit. king's service, here temple service). Some of the latter perform services for temple tenants against cash payments and do not themselves own temple land.

Despite the fact that a number of them are goyigama, the social status of vihara tenants is regarded as somewhat lower than the status of other members of their castes. This does not apply to devale tenants. There is a story about the degradation of a certain section of the goyigama caste by a Sinhalese king, which, for the protection of those involved will not be discussed here. (See Ryan 1953: 217–221, T. M. Seneviratna 1914, and Lawrie 1896–98: 708–709 for other examples of caste degration in Central Ceylon). It is somewhat difficult to explain why people living close to a holy place or doing work for a temple should have a low status. Aiding a temple is usually regarded as meritorious and enhances the karma of an individual. Nevertheless discrimination by other members of the society is widespread, notably in Burma, where at least during the 19th century temple servants had a very low status. A contemporary source describes the situation as follows (Sway Yoe 1882: 427–428):

"the regular servitors of the places of worship, those who sweep the platform, carry off dead leaves, broken branches, and litter generally, and keep the place in order, are not only slaves, but are regarded as outcasts with whom the rest of the community will have no dealings and whose society is contaminating. Not only is the original *parakyun* a slave for life, for no one, not even a king, can liberate him or provide a substitute in his place, but his descendants, till the cycle of Shin Gautama's (the Buddha's) religion shall have come to an end all the relics shall vanish from the earth, all his children throughout the thousands of years that have to elapse, are fixed and settled slaves of the pagoda from their birth, and anyone marrying a pagoda slave, even unwittingly, becomes himself, with all the children he may have had by a previous wife, irremediably a *parakyun*... They are looked upon as unclean, and the rest of the community will have no intercourse whatever with them. So much is this the case that under British rule, which has of course freed them from their compulsory servitude, they are still looked upon with no less aversion than they were when the country was independent..."

In Ceylon the discrimination against vihara tenants was never as strong as in Burma though the temple area as a former settlement of slaves might have its impact on the status of later inhabitants, whether they are direct descendants of slaves or not. Nur Yalman describes a somewhat parallel case in his village of Terutenne in the Nuwara Eliya District, where an area, formerly settled by "serfs", has transmitted its low status connotation to later migrants to the same area (Yalman 1960: 105–108). The rock inscriptions at Lankatilaka mention 200 slaves who were donated to the temple in the 14th century A.D. (Sinhalese Rock Inscription: 19). It is also recorded that to the West houses were built and streets were laid out "for those engaged in the service of the vihara, including male slaves, female slaves, workmen and others..." (Lankatilaka Copperplate C: 2. See Paranavitana 1960a).

Whereas vihara tenants suffer from a depressed status and are often reluctant to admit their connection with vihara service, the devale tenants have no such problems. There is no particular stigma attached to devale service, though temple services connected with very low caste status are often resented (SP I, 1956). The villagers in Hiddaulla, who are predominantly members of the drummer's caste *(beravāyā)*, even show a certain pride in their profession and their connection with a famous temple. This attitude was, however, stimulated by post-independence Sinhalese nationalism, which suddenly made traditional Sinhalese music very respectable and increased the demands for the services of drummers tremendously. They have to attend most public functions or receptions of political leaders to prove the politicians' sincerity in fostering the Sinhalese cause.

Most of the temple tenants are farmers but there are also other occupations to be found among them, ranging from road construction worker to primary school teacher and businessman in Kandy. Even the Mahanayaka Thero of Malvatta (as chief incumbent of the Lankatilaka vihara) holds hereditary rights to some devale land and is thus technically a devale tenant who has to perform temple service. (As will be discussed later, this services consists of chanting *pirit* for the gods). Those tenants living away from the temple villages and following other occupations than farming are usually not active temple servants but employ others to do the service for them.

It is difficult to estimate the total number of temple tenants. Around 1870 there were 79 vihara and 63 devale tenants who shared the responsibility for performing temple service *(rājakāriya)*. I could not establish how many tenants worked temple land which was not subject to rajakariya (*māruveni*, for a detailed discussion see Chapter V). Today the number of tenants has increased substantially due to fragmentation of inherited temple land *(paravēni)*; in 1966 there were more than 200 temple tenants connected with Lankatilaka. The number of active temple servants has, however, not increased as will be shown later.

Whereas temple tenants are clearly separated into those belonging to the vihara and those belonging to the devale system, laymen are not. There are no "Buddhists" as distinguished from "Worshippers of Gods". Though the vihara is more frequented than the devale it is a usual pattern for visitors to worship the Buddha first and to take part in the vihara ritual and then to worship the gods in the devale lateron. The complete absence of sects in the proper sense of the word in Sinhalese Buddhism as well as in Modern Theravada Buddhism in general is a remarkable fact. An explanation will be attempted in Chapter VI.

We have now described the personnel connected with the Lankatilaka temple. The next chapter will be devoted to an analysis of those activities connected directly with the primary function of the temple, the worship and veneration of the Buddha and the seven gods.

CHAPTER FOUR

Religious Organization: Ritual

1. Daily, Weekly and Monthly Vihara Rituals

IN the rock inscription of King Bhuvanaikabahu IV and his chief minister Sēnalankādhikara, dating from the founding of the temple in the 14th century A.D., it is mentioned that "offerings of cooked rice, flowers and lamps to the Buddha and the gods" should be maintained without cessation. A copper plate grant warns those who would cause any obstacle to this that they "will fall into the eight great hells of which the first in Sanjiva, and suffer great torment there, and will not see deliverance therefrom. On the other hand, should there be any persons who will support this by a mere word even, they will obtain the affluence of Heaven and Liberation, and will in the end see the Great Nirvana which is Immortality." (Copperplate G: 8, 18th century A.D.). This warning has been well heeded for almost seven centuries and the offerings are still made today.

There are three types of ritual activities in both the vihara and the devale systems (see Table 10):

(1) The regular rituals at the vihara *(Buddha pūjāva)*, which take place three times a day. The corresponding devale ritual is performed only twice a week, on Wednesdays and Saturdays.

    The regular rituals at the vihara are in addition patterned by the moon calendar. On Buddhist holydays *(pōya, pohoya)*, the fullmoon and quartermoon days, the ritual is slightly more elaborate and attracts more visitors.

(2) The temple festivals. There are four of them per year for both the vihara and the devale, held at the same time.

(3) Other ritual activities, in which the religious specialists of Lankatilaka are involved, but which are not specifically related to the temple.

Though the temple festivals are highlights of religious life and provide entertainment for all villagers in the area, the daily and weekly rituals are clearly the most significant aspects of the religious organization of Lankatilaka. We shall first describe the ritual at the vihara, then those at the devale and attempt an explanatory analysis later in this chapter.

Every morning at about 5 a.m., when the first ray of sunshine appears on a mountain ridge across the Mahaweli Ganga valley, the Buddhist monks in the monastery on the slope of the temple rock and the temple tenants in

Table 10
Ritual Activities at Lankatilaka

Vihāraya		*Devālaya*
	(1) *Regular rituals*	
Buddha pūjāva:		
hildānaya	daily 6.30 a.m.	dēvapūjāva Wed. & Sat. 7.00 a.m.
ahara pūjāva	daily 11.00 a.m.	dēvapūjāya Wed. & Sat. 11.30 a.m.
gilanpasa pūjāva	daily 7.00 a.m.	dēvapūjāva Wed. & Sat. 7.30 p.m.
pasalosvaka pohoya	Fullmoon day	
atavaka pohoya	1/2 moon day	
masa pohoya	Newmoon day	
atavaka pohoya	1/2 moon day	
	(2) *Temple festivals (vihāraya and devālaya)*	
Avurudu mangalaya (New Year 'estival)		April
Äsala perahära (Äsala procession)		Scptember
Kartika mangalaya (Kartika festival of lights)		October/ November
Alut sahal mangalaya (New rice festival)		January
	(3) *Other rituals*	
dāna		gam maduva
pirita		bali
kathina pinkama		huniyam
funeral		

the villages down in the valleys below the temple are awakened by the sound of music. Three temple servants who have passed the night in the *vihāra diggē*, the hall of drummers, join for the *aliyandureya* to remind the officiating bhikkhu and his staff that the morning ritual is soon to begin. They play a drum *(davula)*, a kettledrum *(tamättama)*, and an oboe *(horanäva)* for about three minutes.

A short while later the cook of offerings *(multänrāḷa)* and the attendant *(vatarāḷa)* arrive and enter the kitchen behind the hall *(diggē)*. The vatarala brings some firewood, lights the fire and fetches water, while the cook prepares the food: rice and one or two vegetable curries. Until about 6:30 a.m., the time is filled with a number of further preparatory activities. The ritual attendant opens the doors of the main vihara and of the small shrineroom in the digge. He fills vessels with water and carries them into the viharas, sweeps the floor and sees to it that everything is in order. Other temple tenants arrive. He also arranges white temple flowers on the altar below the Buddha image and lights the candles on the altar. Other temple musicians come along the village foothpath and join those who have already participated in the music *(aliyandureya)* for an early chew of betel and some gossip. The first ritual act is performed by Ananda Samanera, the novice, who comes up from the pansala, carrying a small basket and a piece of leather on which he will kneel while reciting some gathas in front of the Buddha image. He picks flowers from a bush on the temple compound and than offers them in the two viharas, at a small niche in the dagoba, before the two bo trees, and on the Buddha's footprint next to the larger bo tree. The ritual act is very simple and is the same as that performed by lay visitors to the temple, who, however, rarely arrive at this early hour: he worships by putting his raised hands together, and then ordains the place of worship by arranging the blossoms one by one while reciting the appropriate verse.

At about 6: 30 a.m. Buddharakita Thero, the officiating monk, leaves the monastery. The oboe *(horanäva)* player has already taken his position at the eastern veranda of the digge from where he can see the monastery below. As soon as the bhikkhu starts to climb the steep flight of steps up to the temple, the horana player elicits a short melody from his instrument, which with some variations remains his major theme. When the bhikkhu arrives at the temple, the other players have joined in and the music is in full swing. The *hēvisiya* (music, drum-roar) is composed of the sound of the following instruments (see also Coomaraswamy 1956: 26):

(1) *davula*, a common drum, played with one drumstick and one hand.
(2) *tammätan*, a kettledrum, consisting of two small drums, bound together. It is played with two drumsticks.
(3) *horanäva*, a short oboe. The middle part is made of buffalo horn, ornamented with yellow and red rings of lacquer; both ends are made of brass.

Later on, and on special occasions to be described below, the following additional instruments are used:

(4) *beraya*, a long drum, sometimes referred to as rattle drum. It is played on both sides with both hands.
(5) *tamboruva*, a big drum, played on one side with two drumsticks.
(6) *taliya*, brass cymbals.
(7) *hakgediya*, a conch shell which is blown to signal the beginning and end of the ritual proper.

The bhikkhu now walks straight to the main entrance of the vihara without paying any attention to the musicians. After he has climbed up the few steps and disappeared into the temple, the music stops. After a while one of the temple servants takes his position at the temple door and blows the conch shell *(hakgediya)* and then starts to drum on the tamboruva. The other musicians who have been playing before, join in, with a different tune, however. The ritual has started.

The ritual is referred to as *pūjāva* (offering), or, if one wants to distinguish between the vihara and the devale ritual, as *Buddha pūjāva*, offering to the Buddha. The morning ritual is also called *hīldānaya* (from *hīla* = bhikkhu's breakfast and *dānaya* = offering of food to a bhikkhu), of *sisildānaya* (same meaning), after an essential part of the ritual.

The bhikkhu kneels before the principal Buddha image and recites a verse asking permission to perform the ritual *(avassara ganīma)*. After he has finished he prepares the table in front of the principal Buddha image for the first ritual, the *tēvāva*, by sprinkling the altar with perfumed water. He then takes the necessary ritual utensils out of a closet and arranges them on the altar (see Figure 9).

The following ritual is, with minor variations, the same as performed in the Dalada Maligava (A. A. Perera 1920–21: 67–68, Hocart 1931: 18–31) and other royal temples *(raja maha vihāraya)*. (I have witnessed the *tēvāva* several times at Mahiyangana Viharaya and could not detect any major deviations.)

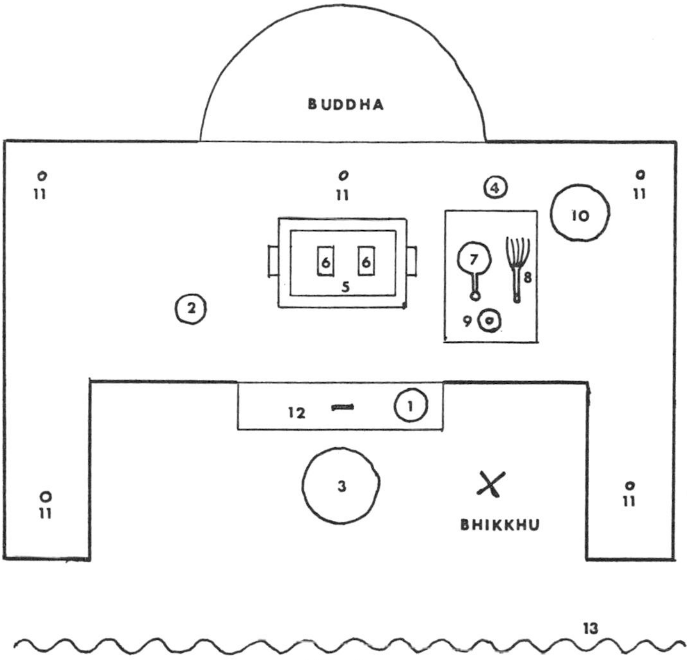

Fig. 9

Tevava at Lankatilaka Vihara

1. Water jar *(keṇḍiya)*
2. Small water vessel *(kusalāna)*
3. Spittoon *(kālañci)*
4. Vessel for scented water *(handun karanduva)*
5. Tray with robes *(atapirikāra)*
6. Towels *(lēnsuva, teta mattuva)*
7. Fan *(vatāpana)*
8. Fly whisk *(cāmaraya)*
9. Bell *(miṇigediya)*
10. Betel tray
11. Candles
12. Box for money offerings *(pinpeṭiya)*
13. Curtain

(1) The bhikkhu holds the large water vessels *(pänkeṇḍiya)* before his head. He then pours water three times into the small bowl on the table and then three times into the spittoon. The water is respectfully called *pän* rather than *vatura* as in everyday Sinhalese.

(2) A toothbrush *(dahatiya)* is then held up and moved back and forth before the Buddha image.

(3) The bhikkhu takes one of the towels *(lēnsuva)*, holds it in his right hand in front of his forehead, and then moves it before the Buddha's

face in circles, his left hand touching his right elbow as a sign of respect.

(4) The same is repeated with the second handkerchief with the difference, however, of waving it somewhat lower close to the Buddha's hands. The last three acts clearly symbolize washing and cleaning of the Buddha's month, face and hands.

(5) The bhikkhu lifts the robes of a Buddhist monk, which are wrapped in a multi-colored cloth, and offers them twice to the Buddha. The packet is sometimes referred to as the *aṭapirikara*, the eight articles required by a Buddhist monk, viz., bowl, two robes, undergarment, girdle, razor, needle, and waterstrainer.

(6) The bhikkhu takes the silver fan *(vatapana)* and slowly waves it three times.

(7) Then he takes the fly-whisk *(cāmaraya)* and waves it forcefully for some time.

(8) The bhikkhu holds up the little bell *(miṇigediya)* and rings it seven times. For this act I cannot offer a precise explanation, except that the ringing of handbells of similar shape is a common feature in all Hindu ritual. The verse which goes with the *miṇipūjāva* (bell offering) refers to the *dhamma* (doctrine, law), which the Buddha expounded "with sweet voice like the sound of a bell." This simile seems, however, a little farfetched at this stage in the ritual and does not really highlight the significance of this ritual act.

(9) The monk lights small pieces of camphor *(kapura)* on a three-armed chandelier, which is then moved back and forth before the image. *(pahan pūjāva)*. This offering is sometimes left out.

(10) The bhikkhu touches the altar three times and worships the Buddha by holding his hands clasped together over his head. Touching the altar substitutes for the offering of a chair to the Buddha on which he is invited to sit for the next ritual act.

(11) The bhikkhu again holds the water jar *(keṇḍiya)* above his head and pours water into the small vessels *(kasulāna)* on the table and then three times into the spittoon. This act stands for washing the Buddha's feet, while he is sitting on a chair.

(12) The bhikkhu kneels on his piece of leather, recites verses, gets up and packs the ritual utensils together, which are then stored away in a locker.

The curtain is now drawn and the *tēvāva* is finished. Up to the point the bhikkhu has been alone in the innermost part of the vihara, hidden behind a curtain. He, as well as other bhikkhus in royal temples, explained that no one else, neither his attendant nor another bhikkhu would be allowed to be present during the *tēvāva*. This rule was indeed strictly observed and it was almost a year before I gained permission to watch the *tēvāva*. Even Hocart, who was Archaeological Commissioner and consequently a powerful official of the colonial government in the 1920's, could not gain access to a tevava at the main shrine of the Dalada Maligava, but was eventually allowed to observe the ritual in another, less important shrine. (Hocart 1931: 19–20).

The next ritual is the *malpūjāva*, the offering of flowers, during which the bhikkhu places some blossoms on the altar. The *hīldānaya* follows immediately. Though access to this part of the ritual is also restricted and usually performed by the bhikkhu alone, the *multänrāḷa*, the *vateruräḷa* or important visitors might sometimes enter and watch the proccedings.

While the other rituals took place, the cook *(mulatänrāla)* has prepared the offerings in the kitchen and filled two small vessels with the rice and the curry. These he puts on a tray, covers them with a colored cloth, and takes them through the digge into the vihara, where he hands the tray to the bhikkhu. The monk puts the tray on the altar and draws the curtain. Then he holds the *keṇḍiya* to his forehead and pours water three times into a small bowl (similar to ritual acts 1 and 11). This water is meant for drinking. He then uncovers the tray, invites the Lord Buddha to partake of the meal and stands back. After a while he covers the tray again, pours the water into the spittoon and leaves the vihara together with the cook or the attendant, who carries the tray and rings a bell near the temple door on his way out. Both go to the lower vihara between the digge and the kitchen and perform the *hīldānaya* in the same way as has been done in the main vihara.

After this the music stops, all doors are locked, the temple tenants go home or to the village boutique at the end of the proccssion street for a cup of tea, and the bhikkhu climbs down to the pansala to have breakfast, prepared by one of the temple boys. The food used for the offerings is thrown away and eaten by dogs and birds.

The ritual as described above is reenacted every morning. It shows the basic pattern for all other ritual. The next daily ritual is the *ahara pūjāva* which is performed at 11 a.m. It consists only of the offering of flowers *(malpūjāva)* and of food *(dāna)* as during the hildana, but there is no tevava. In the evening the so-called *gilanpasa pūjāva* starts again with a tevava, with the minor alteration that the offering of the toothbrush (ritual act 2 above) is left out. The *malpūjāva* is performed as usual. Then during the *gilanpasa pūjāva* proper the tray is not loaded with food but with drinks, usually tea and orange juice. In addition a dish with betel leaves is offered *(dahat pūjāva)*. This is in accordance with the vinaya rule that Buddhist monks should not eat food after noon.

There are two major cyclical variations superimposed on the daily rituals: (1) every Wednesday an additional ritual, the *nanumura mangalaya*, is performed before the ahara pujava at 11 a.m., and (2) some additional ritual directed at Buddhist laymen takes place at fullmoon days *(pasalosvaka)*. Other cyclical events which occur yearly, viz., temple festivals and Buddhist holydays, will be discussed in the next two paragraphs of this chapter.

On Wednesday noon the band of musicians is enlarged by another man playing the long drum *(magul bereya)*. The bhikkhu, who is supposed to have taken a ritual bath, climbs up the temple rock at about 11 a.m. as usual. Before, the rice-offering is carried accross to the vihara, however the *multänrāla* this time brings a tray with one vessel, which contains the *nanu*, a liquid mixed of lime juice and water. When he leaves the *diggē* to cross over to the main temple building, a temple tenant from the washerman's caste (*hēna*) and another temple tenant spread a baldachin *(viyana)* over himself and the tray with the vessel. They then all three walk across to the vihara, followed by the bhikkhu. The two temple tenants only go up to the main temple door, while the *multän-rāla* enters and places the tray on the altar. The bhikkhu then closes the curtain. No one is allowed to be present while the ritual is performed. The secrecy surrounding this part of the ritual is so great that temple tenants are very reluctant to even talk about it though all of them seem to know what is actually going on from hearsay. The importance of the ritual is further enhanced by the fact that it is called *mangalaya*, auspicious festival. The ritual acts themselves are simple enough. The bhikkhu takes the gadgets used for the *tēvāva* and a small mirror with a wooden frame and handle out of a locker. He holds the mirror up so that the Buddha image is reflected in it. First the bhikkhu pours some lime juice over the morrir, then some water out of the *keṇḍiya*. The mirror is then wiped clean with a piece of cloth. After this is accomplished, the *tēvāva* and the *dāna* (as described above) follow. There are, however, some differences. This time, also, the tray with the food offering is covered by the baldachin when carried over to the vihara, and after the *pūjāva* an iron ladle *(dummala-kabala)* with burning incense is brought by the *vatarāḷa* and waved by the bhikk-hu in front of the Buddha image *(suvandadum pūjāva)*. The offering is also more elaborate. Half a bottle of coconut honey, half a bottle of oil, two coconuts and two and onehalf measures of unpolished rice are used to prepare oil cakes and milk rice. It is important to note that these items play a major role in most Sinhalese rituals of purification. (Yalman 1967).

The various verses uttered by the bhikkhu while performing the *nanumura mangalaya*, the *tēvāva*, the *malpūjāva* and the *dāna* are said to be the same as used in the Dalada Maligava. A manuscript in the Malvatta library, transcrib-ed and translated by S. Paranavitana, contains these Pali stanzas (Hocart 1931: 20–31).

On fullmoon days, which are now the official holidays in Ceylon instead of Sundays, the ritual pattern is further elaborated. During the noon pujava more musicians turn up. Two of them play long oboes *(horanäva)*, another uses cymbals *(taliya)*, and an additional drum is played. A number of villagers, mostly women dressed in white sarees (or sarees as white or light colored as possible), assemble at the vihara gate. Some women have brought baskets with flowers or little pots with rice, which they hand to either the multänrala or the vaterurala, who take them inside the vihara and empty them on a big tray and a big bowl standing before the altar. Everyone tries to touch the baskets and pots while they are passed on to the temple servants. Also, when the multänrala comes with the tray of offerings, everyone touches it. The bhikk-hu then performs the pujava as described above. As soon as he is finished and draws the curtain, the people come in to kneel and worship the Buddha by touching the ground three times with their foreheads and laying the palms of their hands together in between. The bhikkhu then recites the Pali verse honouring the Buddha: "Namo tassa bhagavato..." This is also sometimes done by a knowledgeable layman. The visitors sometimes shout "Sadhu" after each verse. The bhikkhu then administers the "three refuges," which are repeated by all laymen:

"Buddham saranam gacchami,
Dhammam saranam gacchami,
Sangham saranam gacchami."(etc.)

(I take my refuge in the Buddha, the Dhamma and the Sangha...) this is followed by reciting the five precepts (*panca sila*):

1. I undertake to observe the precept to abstain from killing living beings.
2. I undertake to observe the precept to abstain from taking what is not given.
3. I undertake to observe the precept to abstain from sexual misconduct.
4. I undertake to observe the precept to abstain from false speech.
5. I undertake to observe the precept to abstain from intoxicating drinks and drugs causing heedlessness.

After this everybody leaves and the temple is closed.

2. Weekly Devale Rituals

In our description of the architectural arrangement of Lankatilaka and in the analysis of temple administration, we have been able to detect the dual character of both. The devale system is in many aspects a replica of the vihara system or vice versa. The same holds true in the case of ritual. The regular religious activities are very similar, though the actors are different. The basic structure of the ritual is the same, though the meaning might differ from the point of view of the actors. (Table 11).

Table 11
Ritual in Lankātilaka Vihāra-Devāle

Vihāra *Buddha pūjāva*	*Devāle* *Dēva pūjāva*	*Major activity*
nānumura (Wednesdays only)	nānumura (Saturdays only)	ritual purification of images
tēvāva	tēvāva	ritual washing and fanning of images
mal pūjāva	—	offering of flowers
dāna	multän bäma	offering of food

The offerings *(pujāva)* at the devale also take place three times a day, but only on Wednesdays and Saturdays. These days are known as *kenmura* days and are observed throughout Udunuwara and Yatinuwara. (See Coomaraswamy 1956: 26. Richard Gombrich informs me that around Teldeniya

Tuesday and Friday are observed as Kenmura days.) The gods are also honoured on these days by lighting small oil lamps posted in an old can or other receptacle on a pole in front of village houses.

The Kandy devales are open to visitors seven days a week. The Lankatilaka devale, in contrast to this practice, is often closed for several weeks. This is justified by the kapuralas and temple officials as necessary to maintain the temple's ritual purity. Death is regarded as highly polluting. Whenever someone has died in one of the temple villages, the devale ritual scheduled for Wednesday or Saturday will be postponed for a week. As death occur frequently the devale stays closed most of the time except during festivals and on other occasions when visitors are expected who are likely to make offerings in cash to the devale or the kapurales. The concern about pollution is used as a justification for keeping onerous temple services at a minimum.

The secrecy surrounding the ritual at the vihara is even stronger at the devale. Spence Hardy, a Wesleyan missionary, who spent over 20 years in Ceylon during the 19th century studying Sinhalese Buddhism, noted that "Europeans are not allowed to enter the dewales, and it is difficult to ascertain the exact nature of the rites therein performed." (Hardy 1860: 201). This rule still applies in regard to the inner chambers of a devale not only for Europeans but also for Sinhalese of lower caste then Goyigama. During the ritual itself only members of the inner temple service are admitted.

On Wednesdays and Saturdays, then, there are deva pujavas in the morning, at noon and in the evening. They follow immediately upon the Buddha pujava on the other side of the temple. On a Saturday morning, when nobody has died the previous week, who might according to the vidanas interpretation pollute the temple, the ritual takes place. The devale musicians start to play as soon as the vihara musicians have stopped. The instruments are the same, but the tunes are different. Even some of the musicians are the same because some devale tenants, who ought to play at the devale ritual, find it easier to pay the vihara musicians who are there anyway all day to perform the services for them. The members of the inner services are, however, strictly separated. While the ritual at the vihara is going on, the *multänrāḷa* of the devale has prepared the offerings for the six gods in the main temple: rice and two or more curries. While working in the kitchen he must follow certain regulations to ensure the ritual purity of the offerings. He must have his long hair covered and wear a clean white shirt which has been washed by a devale dhoby. He should also cover his mouth with a piece of white cloth while stirring the curries and the rice, though I have never seen him actually doing this, but must at least make sure that none of his saliva will drip into the pot. The kitchen is also strictly taboo for women.

The type of food used for the curries is also prescribed. Meat, fish or eggs are not to be used. There are also a number of tabooed vegetables, usually those which are commonly offered to demons *(yaka)* and which have certain attributes, like a powder-covered skin. For instance, ash-pumpkin *(puhul geḍiya)*, ashplantain *(alukesel)* or cabbage *(govageḍiya)* are never offered to gods, though they are favourite dishes of Sinhalese villagers. Also dried salt-fish *(karavaḷa)*, a common ingredient of curries, must not be added to offerings.

First the attendant carries water into the devale, then the *multänrāḷa* follows with the offerings, which he carries in a *hemakadde*. This is a pole with pots suspended from either end. The vessels are covered by draped multicolored cloth.

In the devale the water and the food vessels are placed on a small rough wooden table placed against a wall in a corner. Here the kapurala pours the water into a water jar *(keṇḍiya)* similar in shape but smaller than the one used in the vihara. He then proceeds from shrine to shrine and pours water three times into a receptacle in front of the images of the gods and their consorts. The gods are served in the following order: (1) Visnu, (2) Saman, (3) Kataragama, (4) Vibhisana, (5) Ganapati, (6) Kumara Bandara. The godling Dädimunda Devata, housed in a separate building, is not included. This act, which goes on rather hastily and without any recitation, is called *tēvāva*. It is the equivalent of the rather elaborate ritual of the same name in the vihara. On the whole one has the impression that everybody is mainly concerned "to get it over with." Also the following ritual act, the offering of food *(multän bäma)*, is done without any pomp, and the style in which the gods are served reminds one more of a quickservice luncheonette in a London or New York business district than of an important and solemn religious ritual. The *kapurāḷa* dishes out rice and curry on six plates, standing on the previously mentioned table. He then takes them to the individual shrines, puts them before the images and draws the curtain. After a few minutes the plates are removed and the food emptied into two pots. Special care is taken when God Kumara Bandara is served. The kapurala always looks sideways when he puts the plate with offerings behind the curtain into the srine to make sure that he does not look at the image. Seeing the powerful god would mean instant disaster.

Contrary to the practice of throwing away the food offered to the Buddha, the rice and curry offerings to the gods are later eaten by the temple servants and taken home by some of the visitors. After the food has been removed, water again is offered by pouring it out of the *keṇḍiya* into small vessels in front of the images. The *multänrāḷa* then carries his pots back to the kitchen *(multängē)*, the music stops, and the ritual is concluded by a long deep sound from the conch shell *(hakgeḍiya)*.

The noon pujava on Wednesdays consists just of the offering of food. On Saturdays the tevava and multänbäma is preceded by a *nānumura maṅgalaya*, which is, however, often omitted, allegedly because of purity considerations. I was, unfortunately, never allowed to see a *nānumura*, but the *kapurāḷa* ensured me that it is conducted precisely as in the vihara. The only difference appears in the outer services. While in the case of the vihara ritual a *magul bereya*, an "auspicious rattle drum," is added to the temple instruments, the devala orchestra is enlarged by a drummer and a dancer, who dances and sings praises of God Visnu while the nanumura ritual is performed in the devala. The dancing takes place in the digge where the other musicians also usually play. The evening pujava is a replica of the morning pujava described above.

After each pujava, mainly at noon, some villagers arrive to turn to the gods or one particular god for help. The worshippers are mainly women, but in a few cases a whole family visits the temple. The villagers hand over a small offering of betel and incense sticks to the kapurala and tell him their problems. They also pay the priest a small amount for his services, usually between Rs. –.10 to –.25 (US $ .01 to .03). The kapurala then enters the vihara and puts the offerings on the table or still before the shrine of one of the deities. The person whose request is handled first enters the devale and kneels down, hands clasped in the usual manner of worship. His caste status determines how far he is allowed to penetrate into the temple. "Good Goyigama people" may kneel just behind the kapurala in front of the shrine; a man of the Radala subcaste would usually remain standing. People of lower caste have to remain outside the main devale in the anteroom before a curtain. The major dividing line is apparently between Goyigama and non-Goyigama, similar to the division of temple servants into those of the inner and those of the outer services. In this case the former are Goyigama, and latter are members of lower castes of various description. (See Chapter V:3). The kapurala then chants the request of his client in a singing but urging Sinhalese and makes a vow *(bāraya)* for the fulfillment of the wish. Most requests at Lankatilaka are addressed to Kumara Bandara, whose power to find lost property, to disclose the identity of unknown offenders, or to induce eloped persons to return home, is well known. A typical chant to Kumara Bandara on behalf of a villager goes roughly as follows:

"Respectfully we address you, God Kumara Bandara. The person who is making this request is very poor and very peaceful. He never goes anywhere to harm anybody, he is indeed a peaceful person.

"But my Lord and respected God, yesterday he was working in his field. At that time only his children were at home. While he was away a very bad thing happened. One of his enemies tried to put fire to his house. Luckily he did not succeed, but if he had actually done it the worst might have happened to his children and one might even have died in hospital.

"But I do not know the person that has tried to put fire to the house. I am sorry to say that I have no clue who it might be. But I want to find out that person from among the villagers and it is only you, Lord and respected God, who can find him out. Please do disclose him. I should also like to do something against him. Please break his hands and legs and set fire to his house. When you can do this and clearly point out who the enemy is, this person will come here again after seven days and make an offering to you. If you can do all this as requested I can believe that you are still with us and that you help us, Lord and respected God."

Many requests deal with witchcraft *(hūniyam)*, which someone has allegedly performed against the worshipper, and the god is asked to disclose the person who is responsible for the disastrous effects of huniyam. Among the cases I noted were the following:

(1) A woman claims that someone has done huniyam against her mother who consequently does not feel well. Who has instigated the magic?
(2) A woman relates that they are about to build a new house. She feels that somebody has performed huniyam to obstruct the building operations and bring bad luck into the new house. The identity of the sorcerer should be disclosed.
(3) A woman can't get along with her brother and both are constantly quarreling. She has the impression that the formerly good relations with her brother have been upset by an illwishing person who has performed huniyam against them. Who is this person? A request is made that the god should punish that person by killing him, letting him fall off a high three or letting him drown in deep water.

There are also other cases which do not involve allegations of sorcery:

(4) A man would like to know who has tried to set fire to his house (see above).
(5) A man says somebody has stolen pepper from his garden. He wants to know who did it and wants the thief to be punished.
(6) A woman comes to fulfill a vow *(bāraya)* and brings a small silver image of a man. Her husband had deserted her, but returned after she had made an offering and a vow to Kumara Bandara Deviyo. The silver image is supposed to depict her husband.
(7) A man, his wife and two elder children bring a sick baby, which is placed before the shrine, while the kapurala chants a request to help the child recover. This request is not made to Kumara Bandara, but to Kataragama.

Other requests made to Kataragama were:

(8) To cure a child in hospital, and
(9) To ensure successful return from a trip to Colombo to look for a job.
(10) A woman smashes a coconut on the steps of the Dädimunda Devata Bandara Devale. She does not want to disclose the purpose of her visit but other villagers guess that she is eager to become pregnant.

I have never encountered any requests made to Saman, Vibhisana or Gana.

I did not make, as was originally intended, a complete survey of requests made to gods over a long period or time, but the cases related above make it obvious that almost all requests pertain to a crisis which cannot be solved by ordinary means or are related to conflicts in social relations between villagers which are expressed by accusations of sorcery.

No such requests are ever made at the vihara. Here the concern is with making merit, with enhancing one's chances for a better rebirth. For the villagers the vihara ritual is therefore connected with concern for the next life, which is, however, neither an afterlife nor necessarily nirvana (Ames 1964a). Vihara ritual is also a community affair. Whereas the ritual activities after the deva pujaya are conducted for individuals, the ritual at the vihara is conducted for a group of people who all engage in common activities: chanting the triple gem (the three refuges) and taking the five precepts. People would normally not go to a vihara individually but together with other members of the family or kindred.

So far I have largely refrained from commenting on the various rituals described. In the next section of this chapter I shall attempt to analyse them and venture some tentative explanations. The emphasis will not be so much on symbolism and the relation between ritual and religious beliefs but rather on the sociological and historical significance of the ritual activities in both the vihara and the devale.

3. Analysis of Ritual: Purity and Pollution

During our description of the daily and weekly rituals at the vihara and devale it has become apparent that both are structurally closely related and that both follow the same pattern. The elaborate ritual for the gods is perhaps no surprise because we expect that elaborate ceremonial is bound to surround any "Hindu-type" deity. What really strikes us as unusual is the ritual in the vihara, as Theravada Buddhism is noted for its lack of concern for worldly affairs and the simplicity, rationality and overtness of its ritual. And indeed the usual ritual in a Buddhist village temple is simple enough and has been described as such many times.

What then is the significance of the elaborate ritual at Lantatikala and similar Kandyan temples in Central Ceylon? As we have already noted in our discussion of the architectural features of Lankatilaka, two major cultural contacts have made themselves felt during and after the construction of the temple: those with India and those with Southeast Asia. The first cultural communication system is not problematic. The Sinhalese themselves originally migrated from North India to Ceylon and brought the then-existing Indian culture to the island. Since then the traffic of cultural symbols as well as people has never ceased, though the intensity of the contacts has certainly changed over time. (Raghavan 1964). The relations with Southeast Asia are not as obvious and little research has been done on this topic. (Paranavitana 1929, 1960, 1966). Though I will not present any substantial historical evidence for cultural contacts with these areas I will nevertheless have to make use of these concepts to explain two major themes in present day ritual which are and were intimately connected with these areas: the theme of purity and pollution in Indian caste society and the theme of the Buddhist god-king in South and Southeast Asia.

The concepts of purity and pollutions have been called the "keystone" of the Indian caste system. That this axiom holds true also in the Sinhalese caste system, though perhaps in a somewhat less stringent form as in most Indian societies, has been shown in a number of case studies (Ryan 1953, Ames 1966, Obeyesekere 1966, Yalman 1963, 1967).

Table 12
Ritual Space:
Areas of Different Ritual Purity

Areas	*Degree of Purity*	*Vihāraya*	*Dēvālaya*
Inner	1. very high	Buddha image and altar	Images of gods and their shrines
	2. high	inner part of vihāra during ritual	inner part of dēvāle
	3. high	kitchen	kitchen
Outer	4. medium	outer chamber	outer chamber
	5. medium	hall *(diggē)*	hall *(diggē)*
	6. low	temple compound	

Though Scriptural Buddhism shows little or no concern with ritual pollution, Sinhalese religion viewed as a whole can hardly be understood without the notion of purity and pollution. The Sinhalese pantheon for instance is stratified according to ritual purity (Evers 1964c, Obeyesekere 1966) and Sinhalese ritual is structured by pollution themes (Wirz 1954a).[1] The religious organization of Sinhalese temples, viharas as well as devales, is also effected by the cultural theme of pollution.

Lankatilaka temple itself is divided into fairly clearly marked areas of different ritual purity. Of highest ritual purity are the images of the Buddha and the images of the gods, which are not even touched by the priests themselves. Then follows the inner part of the vihara and the devale, and the kitchens *(multängē)*. Somewhat less pure are the outer chambers of the vihara and the devale. Then follow the two halls *(diggē)*, and finally the temple compound. (See Table 12). One is tempted to compare this arrangement with the cosmological pattern of South Indian or Cambodian temple towns, which with their concentric rings of ritual purity in the form of temple halls, yards and walls depict the universe as well as the religious and social order of the world. We shall later return to this theme.

The ritual purity of these areas is preserved by a number of precautions and by regular purification. The greater the degree of purity, the more severe are the precautions. The temple compound which is clearly demarkated by remnants of an old wall, a partly restored temple gate *(vahalkadde)* and steep slopes

1 The Sinhalese word *kilutu* or *kili* means dirty and filthy in the physical sense as well as polluted in the ritual sense. Though dirt and other stuffs or liquids, like meat or blood, are not only physically but also ritually defiling, pollution can also be affected by events, death, or through contact with a number of defined objects, like meat, dryfish or certain vegetables, and also through contact with low caste people, though villagers are reluctant to admit this.

on several sides, is open to all villagers. In fact a foothpath leading from the road and bus stop to the upper hamlets of Hiyarapitiya, Rabbegamuva and Hidda-ulla runs right across the compound and along the procession street. The only restriction imposed on users of this path is that highly polluting objects, like meat, should not be carried across the temple premises. The kapurala ensured me that a violation of this rule would enrage the gods, who would punish the culprit with smallpox or eye disease within a week.

The vihara and the devale digge are used by the temple musicians who are all of low caste origin. The halls are, however, regularly purified with water and cowdung. There is a special share *(panguva)* of temple land set aside whose tenants are required to effect the purification five times a year. They also have to apply cowdung at the same time to the vihara and the devala floor and to the floor of both kitchens. These areas have to be kept pure and only members of the highest caste are allowed to enter them. This regulation is somewhat relaxed in the vihara, where it applies only during the daily rituals.

The areas of highest purity, surrounding the images themselves, are safe-guarded against pollution by a number of further rules. They may be approach-ed, at least during the daily rituals, only by members of the highest caste, who, however, have to undergo a purification rite themselves before they perform any ritual and who must constantly observe a number of taboos. The rite is simple enough. The bhikkhu is expected just to take a bath before performing the *tēvāva* or *nānumura*, which he would most probably do anyway. The kapurala's purification is a little more elaborate. He has to take a bath, has to apply some lime juice on his head and has to wear a "clean" shirt and sarong, which have been washed by a temple dobhi.[1] The kapuralas must furthermore abstain from eating polluting food, like meat or dryfish. It was somewhat difficult to ascer-tain whether they actually conformed to this rule because most villagers were too poor to afford meat for everyday meals anyway, but they at least upheld the rule in public. The most severe precautions against pollution are taken in the case of death. Here we find an important difference between the vihara and the devale systems. Death pollution is a major concern of the kapurala, but not of the bhikkhu. The Buddhist monk is constantly in contact with death, he attends funerals, visits funeral houses and performs pirit in the family of a deceased person. His robe may even be stitched together from rags found on burial grounds in the case of Dhuttanga monks, though this practice seems to have lapsed today. The kapurala avoids corpses, funerals and funeral houses. He stated that he would not even take a cup of water from a person in whose house somebody had died. The taking of water is usually understood as an indicator of caste status; a person would "not even take water" from another whom he considers to be much lower in caste status. If somebody happens to die in the kapurala's presence he is not allowed to perform any devale ritual for three months, even if his house is purified with cowdung and saffron water,

1 The purification of the king in Kandyan times is alluded to by Knox (1681: 75). He mentions that the king before the Sinhalese New Year celebration starts "washes his head, which is a very great solemnity..."

as is customarily done in all funeral houses. Furthermore the kapurala, is endangered by other polluting events which cannot happen to a bhikkhu, namely the birth of a child and the first menstruation of a daughter. These major polluting events will also bar ordinary villagers from entering a devale, though this restriction lasts for a shorter period. In any case, the kapurala, as well as the devale tenants engaged in the "inner service", have to avoid polluting events. They would usually leave the pollution house until it is purified, and they would purify themselves with water and lime juice.

The division of the temple into pure and impure areas is parallelled by the division of ritual activities into inner and outer services *(piṭakaṭṭalē* and *ätulkaṭṭalē rājakāriya)*. Only those engaged in the inner services are allowed to enter the "pure areas" (1, 2, and 3 in Table 12). This division is also reflected in the basic structure of the Kandyan caste system, which is clearly divided into a high caste, the goyigama, and a number of ranked lower castes[1]. A third group of castes has very low status and is altogether excluded from temple service (Yalman 1967: 60).

The inner services are consequently performed only by goyigama people and the outer services by lower castes. There is great concern to keep this basic distinction in the temple service for the vihara as well as for the devale, but what formerly must have been a powerful ritual of social integration, and a demonstration of the interdependence of the various castes, has now turned into a focus of conflict and resentment, because it makes caste status apparent.[2] The connection between caste and the daily and weekly ritual is as follows: Neither the viharadhipati nor the basnayaka nilame take part in the regular ritual activities. Both are members of the highest goyigama subcaste, the *radala*. This by-and-large endogamous group is the Kandyan aristocracy which formed the administrative elite of the Sinhalese kingdom. It is this function rather than religious status which explains the connection between caste and office in this case. This also holds true for the temple headmen *(vidāna)*, who are appointed by the chief monk and the basnayaka and act as their representatives and administrative assistants. The vidanas are both members of a non-endogamous and loosely defined status group within the goyigama caste, whose name often contains the term "Mudiyanse," or "Mudiyanselagedere." These terms are known as *paṭabändi nama*, form *paṭa* ("strap") and *bändi* ("tied"). "The terms came from a ceremony of "knighting:" the king tied a silken strap around the forehead of a recipient of title. Though originally these were not hereditary titles, there developed in later Kandyan times a whole

1 This division is challenged in the Lowcountry of Ceylon by the Karava and Salagama. The importance of this structural feature for modern Ceylonese society is analyzed in Evers 1964a.

2 My observations differ from Yalman's (1967: 59) who writes: "All the castes I came across in the villages of the Kandyan highlands willingly (sic!) performed their traditional duties at temples and other annual rituals. Caste is so much a part of the villagers' existence that the ethnographer comes to accept it as a permanent feature of the landscape, like rice fields."

subcaste of *mudiyanse* people (*mudiyanse* implying *paṭabändi* title) recruited from the middle ranks of the *goigama* (sic) who gradually constituted a bureaucratic *elite* in Kandyan society." (Obeyesekere 1967: 224, see also Pieris 1956: 173). The vihara vidana from the village of Rabbegamuwa is strictly confined to his role as overseer over temple tenants. The devale vidana sometimes takes part in the ritual and addresses the gods himself. The performance of the *tēvāva* and the *multän bäma* is, however, always left to the kapurala. All other administrative personnel, like storekeepers and keepers of keys, were also goyigama people.

Also in the vihara the ritual is performed by a monk of the goyigama Caste, who is assisted by goyigama attendants. This points to the importance of ritual purity in the performance of the *tēvāva* and the *nānumura* ritual. Only an intrinsically "pure" person, a member of the highest caste, can, after an appropriate purification, perform the ritual. As far as I could make out the *tēvāva* and *nānumura* is only performed at some "Great Royal Temples" (*raja mahā vihāraya*) belonging to the Siyam Nikaya. As this order only ordains members of the goyigama caste,[1] it is somewhat difficult to prove the exclusive connection between caste status, purity and ritual activity in the vihara. The connection is quite definite and obvious in the devale, where the goyigama kapurala even has a myth ready to testify his syperior ritual status. As already mentioned, he claims descent from a distant Brahmin ancestor. The other members of the inner services, the cooks of offerings and the ritual attendant, are also goyigama.

The outer services are performed by members of different lower castes. The baldachin, which covers the offerings and the fluid for the *nānumura* and *pūjāva* at the vihara on Wednesdays, is carried by a man from the washerman's caste (*hēna*). All musicians are from the tom-tom beater's caste (*berevā*) and the devale dancers are members of a *berevā* subcaste, called *näkata*. Other castes provide a number of further services, usually during the festivals.

We have so far shown that purity and pollution are important structural principles in both the vihara and the devale ritual. Purification rites play a major role. The temple itself is divided into areas of differential purity and temple services are performed accordingly by people of different castes and therefore different ritual status. This pattern is clearly connected with similar ones in South India and the social organization of the great South Indian templetowns has most probably influenced the ritual of Ceylonese temples like Lankatilaka.

I will now analyze the ritual acts themselves more closely. The three parts, the offering of food (*dāna* and *multän bäma*), the washing and fanning ritual (*tēvāva*), and the purification (*nānumura*) are clearly distinguished as to their

---

1 The *Dambaḍeni Katikāvata* prescribes that an *upasampadā* candidate has to declare his caste. This has later been interpreted as an indication that only members of the highest caste should be ordained. When the *Syāma Nikāya* was formed, low caste members were still ordained, e.g. Moratota Rajaguru Siri-Dhammakkhandha (Mahanāyaka of Malvatta 1787–1811) was of low caste origin. Today only goyigama are ordained. (I am indebted to H. Bechert for this point).

"sacredness". As Durkheim has already made clear, sacredness is connected with restrictions. The namunura is surrounded by a good deal of secrecy. Nobody except the priest or the monk are allowed to see it and are reluctant to speak about it. The tevava may be seen by high caste temple servants and it is freely discussed. The offering of food is even less restricted. In some viharas the bowl of rice and curry is just placed before the Buddha image for all visitors to see. Flowers can be offered by any laymen at the vihara and the offering of flowers *(mal pūyāva)* by a bhikkhu can be witnessed by anybody present.

The *tēvāva* is a very "naturalistic" ritual. The ritual acts very clearly depict the bathing, washing and clothing of a person. In this way it differs considerably from the usual rituals at Hindu temples, which are made up of a multitude of "symbolistic" acts. The *nānumura*, however, is a ritual of purification, in which the images are symbolically anointed with a liquid which is generally understood to remove pollution. But nevertheless it is at the same time "naturalistic," as it depicts the normal purification any high and pure persons has to undergo: the basnayaka nilame before the perahera, the kapurala before the pujava, and formerly the king, who had to be kept in a state of highest purity. The purity of the king was, indeed, regarded as very important at the Sinhalese court: the king's attendants had to cover their mouths with a piece of cloth when approaching him to avoid pollution of His Majesty's person (Pieris 1956: 9, 16) in the same way the kapurala and multänrala are expected to cover their mouths when approaching the gods.

4. Rites of Identification: the Consecration of the Buddhist God-King

The most striking aspect of the simple ritual, esspecially the *tēvāva*, is that it was performed in the same form consecutively in the vihara, the devale and the royal palace. The palace official in charge of the ritual was called *Diyavaḍana Nilamē* ("waterpresenting officer"). It was his duty to bathe, dress and anoint the king. He was at the same time the chief officer or "temple lord" of the Dalada Maligava. (Pieris 1956: 76). Furthermore, these rituals were performed in the major devales and in the royal temples *(raja maha vihāraya)* connected with a royal capital.

The king himself was awarded both divine status and future Buddhahood. He had to be a Buddhist and his high status was regarded as the result of his good karma, derived from good deeds during former lives. A 10th century inscription proclaims that "none but the Bodhisattvas would become kings of Sri Lanka (Ceylon)" and that they "received this assurance "*viyāran*" from the omniscient Buddha." (Jetavanarama slab inscription of Mahinda IV, 956–972 A.C., E.Z.I: 243, 237. Cited after Rahula 1956: 62. See also Evers 1963: 274.)

On the other hand the king was often addressed as "god" *(deva)*, e.g. Rajasinha II's (1629–1687) "arrogation of god-like attributes to himself was notorious" (Pieris 1956: 11). This divine status was already accorded to Sinhalese kings during the Anuradhapura period of Ceylonese history, but the idea of the godking reached its height during and after the Polonnaruwa period, at about the time Lankatilaka Temple was built (Paranavitana in Ray 1960: 726). The Kandavurusirita, a text describing the daily routine of King Parakramabahu II (1236–1270), relates how His Majesty sits in state on the throne, with all the paraphernalia of royalty and with musicians in attendance, "manifesting the glory of the King of Gods." (Paranavitana in Ray 1960: 728).

We might therefore draw the following conclusions:

(1) An important part of the daily and weekly ritual *(tēvāva* and *nānumura)* is a royal ritual or "state ritual".

(2) The ritual *(tēvāva* and *nānumura)* was identical in the vihara, the devale and the royal palace. Until the downfall of the Sinhalese kingdom in 1815 it was performed in an established sequence before the Buddha, the gods and the king. The interrelation was most conspicuous within the ritual compound consisting of the Dalada Maligava, the royal palace and the Maha Visnu Devale in Kandy. All this brings out and emphasizes the ideological connections, if not the identity, between kingship, Buddhahood and divine status, which is so typical of the Southeast Asian empires of Khmer, Champa, Srivijaya, Majapahit and Pagan. (Heine-Geldern, 1956, 1930; Sarkisyanz 1965).

Though the concepts of purity and pollution are indispensable for an understanding of the rituals, this additional aspect has to be taken into consideration, namely the connection between ritual and political structure. The concepts of purity and pollution point to the cultural complex of India proper. The specific connection between Buddhist and Brahmanical-type religions, however, and the idea of the god-king show a relationship to systems of belief developed to their most spectacular height in Southeast Asia. This particular socio-cultural structure, the combination of the vihara, devale and palace systems, is not necessarily due to direct historical influences from Southeast Asia, but might well be a parallel development based on similar religious and political factors. Further research is I believe, likely to reveal stronger connections between Ceylon and Malaysia, Burma, Thailand, and Cambodia then acknowledged so far. The focus of historical research has unfortunately been either on one particular country or on connections between Greater Indian areas and the mother country, as we have already bemoaned in an earlier chapter.

For an understanding of the present ritual at Lankatilaka Temple, an appreciation of the wider cultural frame of reference in time and geographical space is necessary. During the time Lankatilaka was built and the rituals took shape, the idea of a combined Bodhisattva-God-King role was very much in vogue in Southeast Asia, not however in South India, where Buddhism had disappeared. Ceylon was furthermore cut off from South India through the antagonism and ceaseless wars between Sinhalese Buddhist and Tamil Hindu kings. It is therefore probable that the Sinhalese turned to Southeast Asia to bolster their cultural identity. I would suggest, and this is definitely not more than a suggestion, that under the influence of Southeast Asian ideas of divine Buddhist kingship the three parts of the system—cult of the Buddha, of the gods and of the king—merged more and more during the 13th – 14th century in Ceylon. The temples which used to be separate were now combined in one building, the rituals became identical, though the Buddha himself retained his "Theravada identity'" and the Bodhisattvas were incorporated into the ranks of the gods as Natha and probably also as Saman (Paranavitana 1928–33). The appropriate rituals must have developed during the same period, as the *tēvāva* and *nānumura* are mentioned in the Dalada Sirita, a Sinhalese text of the early 14th century.[1] (Hocart 1931: 35).

I have so far stressed the *structural similarities* between the devale and the vihara ritual and have referred to a third, identical ritual, which did not take place in the temple but in the king's palace. The *tēvāva* and the *nānumura* are not a "service" in the Christian sense. They are not performed for believers or the faithful. In fact, laymen are excluded from the ritual, and will normally not even be present outside the temple when the rituals are performed. There are, however, other rituals performed specifically for laymen, in which worshippers may approach the Buddha directly and the gods indirectly through the priest. In this case both structure and meaning of the ritual and the worshipping is totally different.

Ames (1966: 27–50) has worked out these differences in detail and we cannot but reiterate his argument briefly. The transactions during the rituals can be divided into two categories: reciprocal and non-reciprocal. The interactions between laymen and gods in the devale are primarily reciprocal. The laymen requests through the kapurala a favour in this world: punishment of an enemy, cure from sickness, success in business, love and education (see the first paragraph of this chapter for examples). In return the god is promised a reward or bribe. The ritual transactions between worshippers and the Buddha at the vihara are, in contrast, non-reciprocal. People join the bhikkhu to pledge adherence to the five principles of conduct, they present flowers and rice to the Buddha, which will earn merit *(pin)* and enhance the changes of a better rebirth, but this is not bestowed upon them by the Buddha in return for the offerings. The results are furthermore not expected during the lifetime of the individual and cannot be controlled. In the devale a person wants to strike a bargain, wants to enter into a contract with a god in order to achieve immediate results and to receive services or favours from a powerful agent. In the vihara a person makes a donation without expecting a renumeration directly from the recipient of the gift. Giving without expecting reciprocity enhances one's own

1 Rituals similar to the *tēvāva* are also found in modern Southeast Asia. In Thailand a "ceremonial bathing of the Buddha image" takes place in Buddhist temples, but apparently only once a year during the Sonkraan festival in April (Phya Anuman Rajadon 1961: 93). Maspero (1919: 1–6) describes a ritual in a Cham village temple of Po Nagar in Vietnam, which corresponds to the Ceylonese *tēvāva*, and Aymonier (1891: 232–233) mentions a ritual in another Cham temple (Po Klaun Garai), which resembles the *nānumura*.

moral state and earns merit. Robert Knox has already expressed this in a dictum "Budu for the soul and the gods for this world" (Knox 1681).

One of Ames' informants phrased the difference as follows: "Buddhist giving *(dan dima)* is like presenting "gifts" *(taggas)* to kinsmen and friends, i.e., to one's "equals". Pujava to deviyas is like paying a "bribe" *(allasa)* to someone who is superior—a landlord, headman, government official—in order to enlist his assistance or protection, to ward off his displeasure." (Ames 1966: 34).

Rituals in Sinhalese temples are thus of two different kinds: the *tēvāva* and *nānumura* rituals are identical in the vihara as well as in the devale both in form and meaning. They are basically rituals of purification designed to establish the identity of the Buddha, the King and the Gods. The participation of devotees is therefore unnecessary. The other kind of ritual, the general *pūjāva*, involves the participation of the laity. Here the distinction between vihara and devale system becomes essential. Buddha pujava and deva pujava serve, as explained above, different purposes and different needs. The separation of the two religious systems at the laymen's level thus enables Theravada Buddhist ritual to retain its orthodox meaning, because other more "wordly" religious needs are satisfied by the devale ritual. (Evers 1965).

5. The Temple Festivals

We have so far analysed the daily and weekly cycle of rituals at Lankatilaka, and we have seen that this cycle was modified by the Buddhist moon calendar which superimposed its ritual requirements on the vihara system. The yearly ritual cycle is also a combination and fusion of the vihara and devale systems. The timing of the yearly rituals is, however, determined by the worship of the Gods, to which a Buddhist part has been added in relatively recent times. (Probably as late as the 18th century).

There are four annual temple festivals *(mangalaya)*:

(1) The New Year Festival *(avurudu mangalaya)* in March/April.
(2) The Great Procession *(äsala perahära)* in August/September.
(3) The Festival of Lights *(kācci or kārtika mangalaya)* in October/November.
(4) the New Rice Festival *(alut sahal mangalaya)* in January.

The New Year Festival is a relatively minor affair at Lankatilaka. It consists primarily of a *nānumura mangalaya* at the devale, after which milk rice *(kiribat)* is offered to the Gods. At the vihara larger crowds of villagers tend to turn up bringing offerings and making the pujava more extensive.

The Great Festival takes place in the Sinhalese month of *äsala* (August/September) after the perahära in Kandy which is briefly described in chapter I. It follows the same pattern on a somewhat smaller scale. The main part of the temple festival is the great procession *(maha perahära)* which lasts five days and involves the co-operation of the devale and vihara officials, close to one-hundred temple tenants, up to 15 elephants, and the various religious specialists *(bhikku* and *kapurāḷa)*. Their respective duties will be described in the next chapter on rajakariya (chapter V).

The Festival of Lights is widely celebrated in South and Southeast Asia. It is known as dipavali in South India and loi kratong in Thailand. In Ceylon temples, dagabas and bo trees are lit by small oil lamps which are provided by the temple administration or the laymen. In 1965 the *kācci mangalaya* was celebrated at Lankatilaka on the evening of November 8th. Some temple tenants provided coconut oil and clay lamps as part of their *rājakāriya.* These are placed around the temple, the stupa, the two bo trees and in the digges. At about 6:30 p.m. several musicians assemble before the devale and before the monastery. The chief monk *(vihārādhipati)* of Lankatilaka, Amungama Sri Vipassa Mahanayaka Thero is carried on a chair in procession up the steep temple rock to the vihara. Then the usual tevava is performed in the vihara and in the devale. Meanwhile a large crowd of villagers has gathered, consisting primarily of men in contrast to similar gatherings on fullmoon days which are mainly made up of women. Only men take flowers into the vihara where the Mahanayaka Thero himself offers *mal pūjāva* after the *tēvāva.* After the *gilan passa pūjāva* (evening offering to the Buddha) the kapurala joins the chief monk and both offer flowers at the dagoba. This last act especially demonstrates the integration of the vihara and the devale system, despite the fact that the *basnayaka nilamē* (the temple lord of the devala) has not come to attend the festival (a fact that is widely resented by temple tenants.)

The Theravada Buddhist aspect of this Festival of Lights is that it signifies the end of the rainy season retreat *(vas)* prescribed for monks by the vinaya rules. On the morning of the same day the ceremony of giving robes to the monks *(kathina pinkama)* had therefore taken place. This ceremoney is, however, organised by the villagers and is not a temple festival. At dawn a piece of white cloth is taken to the monastery where the resident monk sews it together in the proper way. At about 10:30 a.m. a small procession, consisting of two drummers, an oboe player, a man carrying a tray with offerings, and several villagers, moves along the foothpath to the pansala, and then after a short rest to the vihara. Here the usual pujava takes place after which the small procession returns to the monastery. Here 12 monks have meanwhile assembled on the veranda, seated in two rows according to their ordination age. Between them various vessels with rice and curry are lined up. Before the monks are served *(dāna)*, a banana leaf is passed around on which every monk puts a handful of rice. This leaf is then taken behind the monastery by a villager and offered to the ghosts *(pretaya)*. After the meal the piece of white cloth mentioned before (which has been made into a robe) is taken in procession with appropriate music to a well next to the pansala, where it is washed by a man from the washermen's caste. The cloth is then placed into a wooden through and the resident monk adds a yellow chemical dye and hot water.[1] The robe, now bright yellow, is put up to dry.

1 Formerly a dye made from yak wood was used. Saffron was never used for dyeing robes.

After a while the monks assemble again in the veranda of the monastery. This time the novices *(sāmaṇera)* are excluded. The new robe is placed on a white cloth between the two rows of monks. One of the laymen then takes the robe and sitting in front of a monk, engages in the recitation of appropriate Pali passages. The monk then stands up and recites some further passages facing another monk. The new robe is then handed around by the monks until it reaches the chief monk *(vihārādhipati)* of the monastery. He stains the robe with a betel leaf and hangs it around his neck. At this moment laymen give cheerful shouts of appreciation. Then one of the laymen pours water into a cup while monks chant. After this an older monks gets up and delivers a sermon in Sinhalese, in which he stresses the importance of the kathina ceremony and the amount of merit one gains from attending and financing it. There is, he says, more merit to be earned from a kathina pinkama then from any other form of offering. If a female gives robes at a kathina she will definitely be reborn as a male. Monks and peasants then rise and return to their home villages.

It is significant that this ceremony takes place at the monastery and not at the temple, and that it is a legal procedure prescribed by the canonical scriptures of Theravada Buddhism.[1]

The connection with the temple ritual and the devale system is only one of time. It is normally, but not necessarily, performed on the same day as the Festival of Lights. (Kaṭhinānisansa n.d.).

The New Rice Festival is a state ritual, insituted by Kirti Sri Rajasingha (1747–1782). Though it takes place shortly after the Hindu festival of Thai Pongal (a harvest festival) its exact timing is determined by the Duruthu full-moon day of the Buddhist calendar.

The festival starts with a blow from a conch shell after which a bundle of coconut flowers—traditional symbols of purity—are taken into the devale. The cook of offerings *(multänrāḷa)* will later place these flowers on some of the devale fields. Then a *dāna* is given at the monastery to the chief monk, his senior pupil and designated successor as viharadhipati, and the other resident monks. After the *dāna*, temple tenants representing the various service shares *(panguva)* of temple lands present betel leaves to the chief monk, as described in chapter III. At about 3 p.m. a small procession is formed by both devale and vihara tenants, some of whom play drums and flutes, others carry flags, while still others just go along. The center of the procession is formed by a kapurala, two temple servants carrying a baldachin which covers a third person who balances a pole with two cloth covered pots *(hemakada)* over his shoulders. These pots will be filled with rice at the royal granary of Gurudeniya and taken back to the devale. The small procession then proceeds through villages and valleys, its flags fluttering in the brisk afternoon breeze and its music

1 I cannot detect any justification for Leach's statement that the kathina ceremony "comes at the end of harvest and part of the ritual plays on the theme that harvested grain is 'dead' seed which must be buried to be born again". (Leach 1962: 96).

attracting spectators along the narrow footpath. As soon as the procession reaches the main road to Kandy, flags, flutes and drums are quite unceremoniously packed into one of the regular CTB buses which takes the priest and the temple servants to Kandy. Here they meet with other temple tenants and musicians from the Dalada Maligava, the four Kandy Devales and other Kandyan temples. At sunset a large perahära of drummers, dancers, elephants, priests and temple tenants proceeds to the village of Gurudeniya about four miles from Kandy, where it is met by several temple lords, including the Diyavadana Nilame of the Dalada Maligava. Inside the storehouse, which is decorated with pure white cloth, rice is measured and distributed to the various Kandyan temples.

The following day the procession returns to the respective temples where the new rice is offered in Buddha and deva pujavas.

Appendix to Chapter Four

6. Pali Gathas recited during the Vihara Ritual

Hocart (1931) has apparently confused the order of the verses and connected them sometimes with the wrong ritual acts. The verses are therefore here given as they appear in the original manuscript. The translation is Paranavitana's and Hocart's with some minor changes (Hocart 1931: 20–31).

1. 'Of courses that have their root is causes, the Tathagato has told the cause; and how to suppress them the great Sage is likewise the expounder.'
2. 'Whether he abides or is extinguished, if the intention is the same the fruit is the same: creatures advance to bliss by what promotes a concentration will.'
3. 'So long, O Blessed One, as thy religion stands in the world, may it abiding receive worship in compassion for the world.'
4. 'Let me anoint with pure, fragrant oil the bull among men, best in the world, of smooth limbs and fair face.'
5. 'On the Sage's golden-coloured resplendent body that conveys sweetness to the eyes of the people I perform the anointing with fragrant myrobolan.'
6. 'Let me anoint the Sage's head with the waters of a golden pitcher, strained clean, mixed with sweet savours.'
7. 'With a thin white cloth scented with clothes-perfume I perform on the Sage's body the wiping off the bathing water.'
8. 'Like the Blessed Ananda Thero let me wash with pure water the Sakyan bull for the salvation of the world.'
9. 'May the Blessed One receive the toothstick and water, as if it were a toothstick of betel vine with the waters of Anotatta.'
10. 'Like the fleeting autumn clouds above, below, round the moon, I perform for thee the wiping of the face with a clean towel.'

11. 'With the triple robe originating from the silken Benares, beautiful with saffron I clothe the blessed Tathagato.
12. 'I give to the Teacher this beautiful, shining, precisious, excellent seat, inlaid with gold and various gems.'
13. 'Lord, I wash Thee adorned with the mark of the wheel furnished with all manner of excellent things, the feet worshipped by gods and brahmas.'
14. 'I honour with fragrant scent the fragrant body and mouth of him who is fragrant with boundless merit.'
15. 'Let me offer this chain of flowers endowed with excellence of colour and scent on the lotus of the glorious feet of the King of Sages.'
16. 'I worship with fragrant smoke endowed with the essence of smell, this excellent receptacle of worship.'
17. 'I worship the Supreme Buddha, lamp of the three worlds, repeller of darkness, with the lamp kindled with camphor and destructive of darkness.'
18. 'Let me honour with a sweet wind-producing fan the Sakyan bull, receptacle of worship, honour, and service.'
19. 'Let me honour the ornament of the three worlds, mine of pure virtues, the successful Blessed Buddha, with a precious fly-whisk.'
20. 'Let me worship with the bell of the Law which the Teacher expounded with a sweet voice like the sound of a bell.'
21. 'Let the Blessed One, onmiscient, free from strains, worthy of offerings, mine of merit, receive the excellent consecrated water. (No. 4 in Hocart's version).'
22. 'Let the venerable Sir in his excellent compassion endure to receive the gruel that is prepared.'
23. 'Let the venerable Sir in his excellent compassion endure to receive the sweetmeats that are prepared.'
24. 'Let the venerable Sir in his excellent compassion endure to receive the food that is prepared.'
25. 'Let the venerable Sir in his excellent compassion endure to receive the curry that is prepared.'
26. 'Let the reverend leader receive this drink, fragrant, cool, suitable, sweet, fair.'
27. 'I invite the Supreme Buddha, the great Teacher, free from passion, I convene the best one on earth, a bull among men.'
28. 'Let the Conqueror receive this betel-mixture provided with leaves of the betel creeper, combined with lime and areca together with camphor.'
29. 'Receive here, Blessed Lord, my offering of flowers, lotuses pink, blue, and white, jasmine, and so forth.'
30. 'Forgive me, venerable World-Sage, Blessed One, the sins I have committed with body, world, thought, by carelesssnes.'
31. 'Let the god rain in due time who promotes the welfare of crops; and let the world rejoice, and let the king be just.'
32. 'Let the gods and nagas of great potency who dwell in heaven and dwell on earth approve this act of merit and long preserve the faith of the world.'

These verses are connected with the rituals described in paragraph 1 as follows:

Verse	1–3	Introduction
	4–6	Nānumura mangalaya
	7–12	Tēvāva
	15–29	Malpūjāva
	30–32	Conclusion

The above verses are composed in somewhat corrupt Pali and are possibly of recent origin.
There are also others, similar gathas, which are used during the ritual. Another such version is given by Arthur A. Perera (1920–21: 67–68).

CHAPTER FIVE

Economic Organization: Temple Lands and Temple Services

1. Temple Lands (Viharagam and Devalagam)

SINHALESE kings have always excelled each other in generosity towards the Sangha and the gods and have donated large tracts of land to both viharas and devales.[1] Lankatilaka also benefitted from the kings' desire to make merit, better their karma and enhance their social status. The Lankatilaka rock inscription of Bhuvanaikabahu IV records the donation of ten villages with 18 yala (= 216 amunu) paddy land and additional highlands right after the construction of the temple was completed in 1344 A.C. (Table 13). This donation was made to maintain the ritual for the Buddha *and* the gods. Further income was provided by the allotment of an import-export tax levied on merchandise bought or sold in the Ceylonese ports. In this case the inscription is very specific: one-third of this tax was to go to the Buddha, one-third to the gods and one-third to the patrilineal descendants of Sena-Lankadhikara, who were to administer the temple. The next land grant of which we have historical evidence, was made by King Vikramabahu III and his *äpa* in November-December 1359 A.C. Two villages, including the Village of Rabbegamuva in the immediate neighbourhood of the temple were this time specifically dedicated for offerings to the principal Buddha image. Later copperplate grants only rededicated some of these villages or repeated the full list. A major gain in the land was apparently effected in the late 18th century, when the village of Arawwawala passed from the aristocratic family of the same name to Lankatilaka vihara. In 1798 A.C. Sri Vikrama Rajasinha, the last king of Kandy, certified the transfer of 5 amunu and 3 päl of paddy land with high lands, gardens and house sites to the vihara.[2] The last account of the temple lands in

1 For an explanation of the religious belief behind this behaviour see Evers 1963. Knox (1681: 116–117) refers to these landgrants as follows:
"Unto each of these Pagodas, there are great Revenues of Land belonging: which have been allotted to them by former Kings, according to the State of the Kingdom: but they have much impaired the Revenues of the Crown, there being rather more Towns belonging to the Church than unto the King. These estates of the Temples are to supply a daily charge they are at; which is to prepare victuals or sacrifices to set before the Idols. They have Elephants also as the King has, which serve them for State. Their Temples have all sorts of Officers belonging to them, as the Palace hath."

2 Lawrie (1896–98: 754) mentions a palm leaf grant *(tudupata)* to this effect which I could, however, not examine. Knowledgeable villagers claim that it is a forgery, and give details, how the transfer was actually effected. As the facts could not be established beyond doubt I shall refrain from relating the allegations.

Table 13

Lankatilaka Landgrants

Village	*Extent of Land*	*Modern Name and Location*	
1. *Inscription of Bhuvanaikabahu IV, 1344*			
	a–p–l		
Alut Badalagoda	72–0–0	Batalagoda	Tank, Ihalavisidere Korale and Hevavisse Korale, Weudawili Hatpattuva, Kurunegala District
Parana Badalagoda	60–0–0	Batalagoda	item
Kasambiliyagoda	12–0–0	Batalagoda	item
Naramgoda	12–0–0	Batalagoda	item
Yakalla	12–0–0	Yakalla	Ihalavisidere Korale West, Weudawili Hatpattuva, Kurunegala District
Kirivavula	12–0–0	Kirivavula	Medapalata ,Udunuvara, Kandy District
Gonvanika (in Sitdavulla)	12–0–0	Hiddaulla	item
Deltota	12–0–0	Deltota	Gandahe Korale South, Pata Hewaheta, Kandy District
Godavela	12–0–0	Godavela	Kandukara Palata, Pata Hewaheta, Kandy District
Santana	(forest)	Hantane	item Pata Hewaheta, Kandy District
Total	246–0–0		
2. *Alavala-Amuna Inscription of Parakramabahu V, ca. 1344–1359*			
Alut Badalagoda } Parana Badalagoda } Kasambiliyagoda } Naramgoda }	1080–0–0		(as above)
Siddaulla }	36–0–0		Hiddaulla, Medapalata, Udunuvara, Kandy District
Gonvanake }			
Kirivavula }			(as above)
Godavela }			(as above)
Other villages	84–0–0		
Total	1200–0–0		
3. *Inscription of Vikramabahu III, 1359*			
Pattiyegama (Godarata)	?		Pattiyamulla(?), Gandahe Korale S., Pata Hewaheta, Kandy District
Rabbogamuva	?		Rabbegamuva, Medapalata, Udunuvara, Kandy District

4. *Copperplates, 18th Century*		
(Same as above 1 & 3)		
Godavela	?	(as above)
(rededicated by Kirtti-Sri Rajasimha in 1767)		
Rabbegamuva	?	(as above)
(rededicated by Rahadhirajasimha in 1787)		

Source: Inscriptions and copperplates. Text reprinted and translated in Paranavitana 1960.a

Kandyan times is given in the *hī lēkam mitiya*, a register of ploughed lands, which was compiled about 1810–11. (Report of the Temple Land Commissioners 1857–58: 6). According to this register Lankatilaka vihara had 71–3–3 amunu (about 143 acres) of paddy land and the devale owned 32–1–0– amunu (about 64 acres). Highlands are not registered in the register of ploughed lands of the Kandyan Kingdom *(hī lēkam mitiya)*. Between 1359 and 1810 lands in the Kandyan lowcountry had slipped from the temple lords' control, probably in times of political instability. A further reduction of temple property may have occurred in early British times when comissions were set up to register temple lands. As temple villagers did not pay taxes in kind, cash or labour to the government, the temple land commissioners did their best to reject as many claims to temple land as possible. Almost half of the land claimed by both Lankatilaka vihara and devale was not registered by the temple land commissioner in 1857–58. (Table 14). The registration of temple lands and services had, however a very stabilizing effect on the system. Once certificates had been issued and the services connected with the temple lands put down in writing, the mighty judiciary machine of the colonial government could be used to maintain the status quo. The extent of viharagam and devalagam is therefore today, 1964–66, more or less the same as in 1857.

The temple lands which are still owned today are all situated in the vicinity of the temple, within a radius of four miles. The temple lands in the Kurunegala District have all been lost. Paranavitana (1960a: 39) visited the

Table 14

Lankatilaka Temple Lands Registered 1857–58

	Fields		*Highlands*		*Total*
	registered *a–p–l*	*rejected* *a–p–l*	*registered* *a–p–l*	*rejected* *a–p–l*	*claimed* *a–p–l*
Vihāragam	49–3–9	29–0–1*	185–3–1	92–0–9*	357–0–0
Dēvālagam	24–3–0	13–2–2	0–0–0	105–1–1	143–2–3
Total	74–2–9	42–2–3	185–3–1	197–2–0	500–2–3

Source: Report of the Temple Land Commissioners 1857–58: 25–50.

* Rejected claims in Udunuvara only. The extent of claims on viharagam in other divisions, if any, has not been ascertained.

area in 1931 to register the Alavala-Dam stone inscription which relates the dedication of these lands to Lankatilaka temple. The villagers then told him, that, according to local tradition, the inscription referred to a land grant to a vihara nearby. The original connection with Lankatilaka had been forgotten.

Most of the present land was apparently dedicated right after the building of the temple in 1344. Though no absolute proof is possible, a comparison between the medieval land grants and the present landholdings indicate that the latter are fractions of the original temple lands. The present devale village of Hiddaulla situated East of Lankatilaka is most probably identical with the *Sitdavulla* of the Sinhalese rock inscription of 1344 and the *Siddaulla* of the Alavala-Amuna inscription of ca. 1350. (H and S are easily interchangable in Sinhalese). Most of the devalagam is found at Hiddaulla. The viharagam at the village of Pamunuva is apparently part of the formerly more extensive gama of *Kirivavula* mentioned in the inscriptions. *Rabbegamuva*, where most of the vihara fields are situated, was dedicated to the vihara in 1359 and *Godavela* on the other side of the Mahaveli Ganga was granted, together with forests of Hantana (Santana in the inscription), as early as 1344.

The lands at Hiyarapitiya, Tirappuva and Daulagalla might be later additions not mentioned in any of the stone inscriptions or they may have originally formed part of the templelands at Rabbegamuva. The only present temple lands which were not already dedicated to the temple in the 14th century are therefore those of Arawwawela, a major vihara village south of Lankatilaka. This village was formerly nindagam and belonged to the third system mentioned above. Altogether the lands attached to Lankatilaka temple amount to more than 260 amunu (approx. 520 acres) of paddy fields and highlands. (Table 15).

Temple lands are divided into two basic categories:

(1) *baṇḍāra* lands and
(2) *paravēni panguvas.*

Table 15
Baṇḍāra Lands and Paravēni Pangus of Lankatilaka Temple

		Fields *a–p–l*	*Highlands* *a–p–l*	*Total* *a–p–l*
Vihāragam	Baṇḍāra lands	24–2–3	152–0–8	176–3–1
	Paravēni pangus	25–1–6	33–2–3	235–3–0
	Total	49–3–9	185–3–1	235–3–0
Dēvālagam	Baṇḍāra lands	n.i.*	n.i.	
	Paravēni pangus	24–2–4	—	24–2–4
	Grand total	74–2–3	185–3–1	260–1–4

* Approx. 1–2–5. See footnote 1 on page 78.

The *baṇḍāra lands* are the absolute property of the vihara or the devale.[1] They consist of

(a) the temple compound and the site of the pansala,
(b) the *muttettuva*, paddy fields which normally are cultivated by tenants of certain paraveni pangus. The whole produce goes to the temple, and the temple lords, The *vihārādhipati* and the *basnāyaka nilamē* are supposed to use the income for the maintenance of the temple, administrative expenses and certain rituals or temple festivals.
(c) *maruvena panguvas*, shares of temple land which are leased to tenants for a threeyear period against payment of half the crop to the respective temple lord *(andē)*.[2] Originally the tenants of maruveni pangus seem to have been obligated to perform specified services *(rājakāriya)* for the temple, or bring supplies, often oil for lamps.

The *paravēni paguvas* are owned by villagers themselves who must, however, perform services *(rājakāriya)* for the temples. Economically the paraveni pangus are less important today for the temple than the bandara lands, but for the ritual activities of both temples the paraveni nilakariyas (tenants) are indispensable. Tenancy of paraveni pangus is therefore primarily paid for in labour and partly in supplies which are, however, usually not part of the produce of the land. Bandara lands yield direct income from the produce of the land in cash or in kind. The important aspect of this difference is that the use of the benefits derived from paraveni lands is predetermined. Income from paraveni pangus is immediately transformed into expenditure. A tenant of a paraveni pangu has, for example, to appear at the temple three times a day to drum, and the "income" of the temple, the service of a drummer, is immediately "consumed" for ritual purposes. The payments in kind from nilakarayas (tenants of paraveni pangus) are also determined for immediate consumption. Nilakarayas must, for example, bring oil for the karthika festival, which is immediately used to light the lamps necessary for the festive occasion.

The bandara lands, in contrast, allow *capital formation.* The major part of the income is de jure destined to defray extra costs of temple festivals to pay for the temple administration and, in the case of the vhihara, the living expenses and the education of bhikkhus. However, a concentration of funds over years, their tranfer temporarily or permanently to other purposes is de facto possible. Facts and rumours about the use of these funds for business ventures or political expenditures in the widest sense of the term are well known in Ceylon, though this does not, of course, mean that all temple funds are misappropriated or that the temple lords of Lankatilaka are necessarily engaged in such practices.

The income of Lankatilaka vihara from bandara lands is considerably higher than that of the devale. In the 1960's the *officially* declared income of the

1 The extent of bandara lands is difficult to ascertain as "at no time have registers been prepared" (SP I, 1956: 27).

2 Payment of half the crop is a violation of the Paddy Lands Act, which prescribes that only a quarter of the harvest has to be rendered to the landlord.

vihara from these lands was about Rs. 22, 500, that of the devale only Rs. 950 per year. The devale muttettuvas are still worked by paraveni tenants, but the vihara muttettus are now all given in ande (against a fixed share of the harvest) to tenants and are held on the same basis as maruvena pangus. This change was made in the 1940's during World War II. The viharadhipati found that the income from muttettus was higher when tenants received half the produce of the land than when it was reluctantly cultivated by nilakariyas as part of their rajakariya and the whole harvest went to the vihara. Some of the rents for highlands are paid in cash by a tea estate which holds viharagam, but the major portion of the income is still derived from the sale of paddy, tea, coconuts and kurakkan from bandara lands. Table 16 gives an estimate of

Table 16

Estimated Income from Bandara Lands and Offerings and Estimated Expenditure of Lankatilaka Temple

Income	*Vihara* Rs.	*Devale* Rs.
1. Rents *(badu mila)*	1,532	—
2. Paddy	6,720	950
3. Coconuts	360	—
4. Tea	11,040	—
5. Kurakkan	2,250	—
6. Other products	576	—
7. Offerings	—	50
Total Income	22,478	1,000

Expenditure	*Vihara* Rs.	*Devale* Rs.
1. Maintenance of buildings and roads	600	—
2. Furniture	-	20
3. Lighting	490	75
4. Food, medical attendance and clothing of bhikkus, feeding of attendants and nilakarayas	4,560	—
5. Offerings to the Buddha or the gods	365	40
6. Temple festivals	800	725
7. Salaries and wages	1,860	25
8. Wages for tea plucking, etc.	7,870	—
9. Travelling expenses of chief monk and basnayaka nilame	240	45
10. Stationary, postage, etc.	100	5
Total Expenditure	16,885	935
Balance	5,593	65
	22,478	1,000

Source: Unpublished records in the Public Trustee's Office, Colombo, for 1962–1966.

income from bandara lands in 1962 as declared to the Public Trustee in Colombo. The total income is difficult to ascertain, because the home consumption, the services of nilakarayas and other incomes, vary and are not easy to evaluate. The value of rajakariya services was fixed by the Service Tenure Commissioner in 1870 as Rs. 768.65 per year for the vihara and Rs. 735.35 for the devale. Since then wages have gone up considerably and the labour due to the temple is worth much more. On the other hand, many of the services have become obsolete and are no longer performed. The exact money equivalent of the services is relatively unimportant. Their social and ritual value is more significant. I will therefore concentrate on these services in the following section.

2. Temple Lands Subject to Temple Service

A paraveni panguva is "an allotment or share of land held in perpetuity by one or more holders, subject to the performance of certain services. Such a pangu generally includes paddy fields and gardens, appurtenant to the dwellings, and chenas" (highland unable for shifting cultivation). (SP I, 1956: 2). It is also regarded as a unit of contribution of service. The tenants are called *nilakārayā* and the service *rājakāriya*, literally "king's work."[1] The latter term described all services due to the king and his officials by citizens of the Kandyan kingdom and now means "government service" in modern Sinhalese as well as in other Southeast Asian languages. Though the temple lands are scattered through eight different villages (Table 17) they are nevertheless regarded as one joined *gama* (estate) for each section of the temple. We thus have a *vihāragama* and a *dēvālagama*. The people, having ancestral *(paravēni)* rights in the temple "estates," *(gama)* form a group, the structure of which is made apparent in their interrelated services *(rājakāriya)* to the temple. The temple is therefore the focus of a social structure which cuts across village boundaries.[2]

The viharagama as well as the devalagama is divided into shares *(panguva)*, which are subject to a specified number of temple services. The extent of land of each pangu and the services attached to them were recorded in great detail by the service tenure commissioners around 1870. As their records are still used today to determine the rajakariya of nilakariyas, and as a comparison between the lists used by the vidana of the devale today and the service tenure register of 1872 has revealed only minor differences, we shall use the register as base material for our analysis. Deviation from the prescribed norms will be discussed from time to time.

The devalagama is divided into two parts, the *gamvasama* and the *nila pangu* or nilavasama. Gamvasama was in Kandyan times land held by village headmen *(gamarāla)* (Pieris 1956: 236, Obeyesekere 1967: 223, Codrington 1938)

1 For a description of the rajakariya system in the Kandyan Kingdom see Pieris 1956 and the references cited in this study.

2 Compare also Obeysekere 1967: 13–14, who discusses the meaning of *gama* and *paraveni* at some length in another context.

Table 17
Lankatilaka Temple Villages and Temple Lands
(Paraveni pangus, subject to rājakāriya)

Village	*Vihāragagam*				*Dēvālagam*			
	Fields a–p–l	*Gardens a–p–l*	*Chenas a–p–l*	*Total a–p–l*	*Fields a–p–l*	*Gardens a–p–l*	*Chenas a–p–l*	*Total a–p–l*
Hiddaulla	—	—	—	—	19–1–3	—	—	19–1–3
Pamunuva	1–2–0	1–2–0	—	3–0–0	—	—	—	—
Rabbegama	8–0–9	10–3–4	10–0–3	29–0–6	1–1–0	—	—	1–1–0
Hiyararapitiya	0–3–2	0–1–7	—	1–0–9	1–1–0	—	—	1–1–0
Tirappuva	1–1–5	0–0–6	—	1–2–1	2–3–1	—	—	2–3–1
Arawwawalla	5–1–6	2–2–2	4–1–7	12–1–5	—	—	—	—
Daulagalla	2–0–0	0–3–6	1–3–0	4–2–6	—	—	—	—
Subtotal	19–1–2	16–1–5	16–1–0	51–3–7	24–2–4	—	—	24–2–4
(Udunuvara) Godawela	6–0–4	0–3–8	—	7–0–2	—	—	—	—
Total	25–1–6	17–1–3	16–1–0	58–3–9	24–2–4	—	—	24–2–4

Summary:

Lankātilaka Vihāraya:	Fields	25–1–6
	Highlands	33–2–3
	Total	58–3–9
Lankātilaka Dēvālaya:	Fields	24–2–4
	Grand Total	83–2–3

Note: There is a difference of 2 las for Rabbegama viharagam fields between the figure given here and the figure given in the Report of the Service Tenures Commissioner for 1872, pp. 483–497. The figures in this table have been directly compiled from the original manuscript of the Service Tenure Register of 1872.

and by people whose main duty was to provision officials on circuit (Pieris 1956: 116) They were generally the wealthiest farmers in a village and held the most fertile lands (Coomaraswamy 1956: 24). Today gamvasamas are still found in villages in the Northern Dry zone, where a share of irrigated land behind a tank is reserved for the gamarala. Leach (1961: 166–167) notes that in his village of Pul Eliya "the owner of this strip is automatically entitled to call himself gamarala, though today there is no advantage in doing so." The holder of a gamvasama is, however, under obligation to play a leading role in annual rituals. (Leach 1961: 167). At Lankatilaka the gamvasama is also connected with leadership functions in the rajakariya system. There are five different pangus, held by so-called *mahapangukārayo* ("great shareholders"). Each mahapangukaraya has supervisory functions, like taking account of the offerings, superintending the work of nilakariyas, measuring the seed paddy given out of the devale storehouse to tenants, or reaping the first sheaf of paddy on the devale muttettuva. These functions are indicated in the names of the pangus which can be roughly translated as the Great Official Land, the Storekeeper's Official Land, the Measurer's Official Land, the Messenger's Official Land and the Overseer's Land. It is certainly no coincidence that there are exactly *five* shares. "In the Kandyan royal villages *(gabadāgam)* of Uva ... there were generally five *paṭabändō* ... the principal hereditary tenants, and in Vellassa the coheirs of the *gamarāḷa* in the *māruvena gamvasam* villages, the *pangu-kārayō*, also were five in number." (Codrington 1938: 2). The well-known Indian institution of the panchayat, the village administration by a council of five, might have provided the model for the division of the gamvasama into five shares.[1] The five shares of the gamvasama are about equal in size, between one and one and one-half amunu. Four of them are located in the village of Hiddaulla, one in Tirappuva. (Table 18).

Table 18

Lankatilaka Devalagama, Service Shares and Tenants' Caste

Name of panguva	*Extent a–p–l*	*Village*	*Caste*	*(Sub-caste)*
Gamvasama				
1. Gepalāna Gamvasama (Temple Master's Official Land)	1–1–1	T	Goyigama	(M)
2. Mahagamvasama (Great Official Land)	1–2–8	H	Goyigama	
3. Mānagamvasama (Measurer's Official Land)	1–0–5	H	Goyigama	
4. Payindakiyana Gamvasama (Messenger's Official Land)	1–2–0	H	Goyigama	(T)
5. Dura Panguva (Overseer's Share)	1–1–0	H	Goyigama	
Nilavasama				
6. Kapu Panguva (Priest's Share) (Ranayudha Panguva=Golden Weapons' Share)	1–2–4	H	Goyigama	(B)
7. Multän Panguva (Foodofferings Share)	0–2–0	HY	Goyigama	(T)
8. Uḍavikarana P. (Assistant's Share)	0–2–0	H	Goyigama	(T)
9. Ätulkattalē Nilapanguva (Inner Service Sh.) (Hakgeḍi Panguva=Conch Shell Share	2–0–6	H	Goyigama	(T)
10. Ätulkattalē Nilapanguva (Inner Service Sh.) (Mutukuḍē Panguva=Pearl Umbrella Share	0–1–2	H	Goyigama	
11. Mutukuḍē Panguva (Pearl-Umbrella Share)	0–1–6	H	Goyigama	
12. Palihana Panguva (Shield Share)	0–0–6	H	Goyigama	
13. Talapat Panguva (Palmyra-Umbrella Share)	0–1–8	H	Goyigama	

1 Panchayat-like councils were also common in ancient Ceylon. (EZ I, 8:18; EZ II, 6; Codrington 1938:2).

14. Badahäla Panguva (Potter's Share)	1–1–0	H	Badahaḷa	
15. Rada Panguva (Washerman's Share)	1–1–0	HY	Henaya	
16. Davul Panguva (Drum Share) (Hēvisi Pangu=Drumming Share)	1–1–0	R	Batgam Durayi	
17. Tammätan Panguva (Kettle-Drum Share) (Hevisi Pangu=Drumming Share)	0–3–8	H	Beravaya	
18. Horanä Panguva (Oboe Share)	0–3–0	H	Beravaya	
19. Nätun Panguva (Dance Share)	1–2–0	T	Beravaya	
20. Koḍi Panguva (Flag Share)	0–0–6	H	Padu	
21. Nila Panguva (Service Share)	3–1–0	H	Padu	
22. Gomamatigana Panguva (Cowdung Share)	0–0–4	H	Padu	
23. Pirit Panguva (Pirit Chanting Share)	1–1–0	H	Goyigama-Buddhist Monk	(R)

Abbreviations:

Villages: H = Hiddaulla
HY = Hiyarapitiya
R = Rabbegamuva
T = Tirappuva
Subcastes: B = Bamunu Kule ("Brahmin descent")
M = Mudiyanse (Kandyan traditional officials)
R = Radala (Kandyan Aristocracy)
T = Timbili

The nilavasama is divided into 19 shares *(panguva)*, which can be grouped into six entities. Each group of shares is held by members of a particular caste, who have to perform at least some caste-specific services. This resembles the organization of the Kandyan administration into "departments" *(badda)*, each of which consisted of members of a particular caste and the land they held for their services to the government (Davy 1821).

The pangus vary in size from six las to almost three amunu and are scattered throughout the four temple villages of Hiddaulla, Tirappuva, Hiyarapitiya and Rabbegamuva. The first group of pangus is held by members of the goyigama caste and is connected with the ritual activities inside the devale. The tenants are the "religious specialists" and their assistants described in Chapter III: the priest *(kapurāḷa)*, the cook of offerings *(multänrāḷa)* and the ritual attendant *(vatarāḷa* or *vaterurāḷa)*. The pangus are called accordingly *kapu panguva* (priest's share, also called *ranayudha panguva* or golden weapon's share, because the kapurala has to take the weapons or insignia of the gods in procession from the devale to the sinhasena during the main festival), *multän panguva* (food-offering share) and *udavikarana panguva* (attendant's share). Intimately connected with these three pangus are five others which are also held by goyigama people, two *ätulkaṭṭalē nila pangu* (inner chamber service shares), the *mutukuḍē panguva* (pearl umbrella share,) the *palihana panguva* (shield share) and the *talapat panguva* (palmyra-umbrella share).

The *ätulkaṭṭalē nila pangu* are also known as *hakgedi panguva* (conch shell share) and *mutukuḍē panguva* (pearl umbrella share). All the objects which designate these pangus are associated with auspiciousness, ritual purity and royal status—three concepts which are very much connected in Sinhalese state ideology. Contemporary drawings show the last king of Kandy, Sri Vikrama Rajasinha, attended by his chief officials, some of whom hold the three insignia of royalty, the mutukunde, the paliha with the sun-design, and the talapata. These insignia are also carried in the festival procession of the gods by tenants of the respective shares. (See also the illustration of "A Kandyan Disava and Priest of Boodhoo"—most probably a Mahanayaka Thero—in Davy 1821).

The second group of pangus is held by members of service or artisan castes, washerman *(hēnaya* or *radavā*) and potters *(baḍahälayā)*. In the case of larger temples a number of other artisan shares might be found, e.g. a smith's share. In our discussion of ritual (Chapter IV) we mentioned the important function of washermen. The rajakariya of the potters, the supply of pots, is also highly significant in Sinhalese ritual (Yalman 1963).

The third and very important group of pangus is connected with temple music and is held by members of the so-called tom-tom beater's or drummer's caste *(berevāyō* or *näkati*). One pangu is held, however, by padus from Rabbegamuva. The pangus are named after the instruments which the tenants play: *hēvisi* (drumroar) or *tammätan panguva* (kettledrum share), *hēvisi* or *davul panguva* (drum or tom-tom share), *horanä panguva* (aboe share) and *nätun panguva* (dance share). The fourth group consists of three pangus, which are held by members of the *batgam durayi* caste, about whom more will be said later. Their major rajakariya is to carry the devale flags in the processions of temple festivals, and to clean the devale floor ritually with cowdung.

There is one panguva left which does not fit into any of the group mentioned so far, the *pirit pangua* (chanting share). It links the devale to the vihara and is owned by the latter. The chief monk and incumbent *(vihārādhipati)* has to chant *pirita* for the gods during the perahära as rajakariya attached to his panguva. Thus the Mahanayaka Thero of Malvatta is therefore technically a temple tenant *(nilakārayā)* of Lankatilaka devale. He does, of course, not work the land himself but sublets this fairly large panguva of more than one amuna to a tenant on a half-share basis *(andē)*.

The whole devalagama is thus divided into two parts, the gamvasama and the nilavasama, each of which consist of a number of shares *(panguva)*. The nilavasama is again divided into four groups of pangus, which differ in the type of rajakariya attached to them and in the caste affiliation of their tenants. The pangus themselves consist of one or more fields *(kumbura)* each, which have individual names and do not necessarily lie adjacent to one another. They are in fact situated in different villages in some cases, which indicates that the devalagama and the pangus are understood mainly as theoretical or abstract entities and not only as physical or geographical ones. The gama and the pangus are primarily units of service *(rājakāriya)*, organized and patterned after an ideal model. We might speculate that the model was developed in the dry zone of Ceylon during the "classical" period of Sinhalese history. The rice lands behind a dam, served by irrigation channels issuing from a reservoir, were regarded as one gama. This estate was divided into pangus for the purpose of distributing scarce irrigation water, on the one hand, and allotting specific services for the common good, like maintenance of irrigation works, places of worship and the central administration, on the other. Indeed the available descriptions of the organization of dry zone agriculture (Ievers 1899, Codrington 1938, Pieris 1956: 236–240, Brohier 1934–35, Leach 1964) make it plausible that the basic structure of temple estates was developed in an area where the ecological conditions were quite different from the Kandyan highlands.

The Lankatilaka viharagama is evidently patterned after the same model, but the structure is less rigid. The arrangements of the pangus and the appropriate services appear not to be as fixed as in the case of the devalagama. Using again the service tenure register of 1872 as basic material, we can discern the basic structure of the viharagam by using the model of the devalagam as our guideline. (Table 19).

Table 19
Lankatilaka Viharagama

Name of Panguva	*Fields a–p–l*	*Extent Garden*	*Highld. a–p–l*	*Village*
Gamvasama				
1. Migondena Panguva (Buffalo Share)	1–2–2	0–0–6	0–0–0	A
2. Migondena Panguva (Buffalo Share)	0–0–0	0–2–6	0–0–4	R
3. Payinda Panguva (Messenger's Share)	(maruvena)			G
4. Dura Panguva (Overseer's Share)	1–0–2	2–3–1	3–3–2	R
Nilavasama				
5. Multän Panguva (Food Offering Share)	0–2–4	0–0–5	0–0–0	A
6. Multän Panguva	(maruvena)			P
7. Multän Panguva (Mutukuḍē Panguva=Pearl Umbrella Sh.)	0–3–5	0–0–0	0–0–0	T
8. Nila Panguva (Service Sh.) Malmura Panguva=Flower Service Share)	0–1–2	0–1–2	0–0–0	HY
9. Rada Panguva (Washermen's Share)	0–0–0	0–0–5	0–0–0	HY
10. Hēvisi Panguva (Drum Share)	0–2–0	0–0–0	0–0–0	HY
11. Hēvisi Panguva (Drum Share)	0–2–0	0–0–6	0–0–0	T
12. Horanē Panguva (Oboe Share)	0–3–4	0–0–8	0–0–8	R

13. Nila Panguva (Service Sh.) (Kodi Panguva=Flag Share)	6–0–4	0–3–8	0–0–0	G
14. Nila Panguva	2–0–0	0–3–6	1–3–0	D
15. Nila Panguva	1–2–0	1–2–0	0–0–0	P
16. Dodanangē* Nila Panguva	1–0–4	2–1–6	1–0–6	R
17. Bokumburē Nila Panguva	1–1–0	0–3–2	1–0–6	R
18. Moragahakumburē Nila Panguva	0–3–0	1–2–3	2–0–3	R
19. Pallegorakē Nila Panguva	1–0–0	1–1–6	1–1–2	R
20. Kahatagahaḍeniyē Nila Panguva	0–3–0	0–2–0	0–1–8	R
21. Puvakdandāvē Nila Panguva	0–2–2	0–1–0	0–0–5	R
22. Pussēyatta Nila Panguva	0–1–6	0–0–0	0–0–0	R
23. Asväddum Panguva (New Field Share)	0–2–3	0–1–2	0–0–0	R
24. Hēn Panguva (Highland Share)	0–0–0	0–0–0	0–1–4	R
25. Nila Panguva (Service Share)	3–1–0	2–1–7	4–1–7	A
Total extent of viharagama (paraveni pangu)	25–1–6	17–1–3	16–1–0	

Source: Service Tenure Register of 1872, Kandy District. Ms. in the Kandy Katcheri.

* 16–22. Here the names of the major paddy fields are mentioned in the Service Tenure Register to designate the otherwise undifferentiated nila pangus. This practice is also followed today.

Abbreviations:

Villages: A = Arawwavala; D = Daulagala; G = Godavela; HY = Hiyarapitiya; P = Pamunuva; R = Rabbegamuva; T = Tirappuva

There is again the division into *gamvasama* and *nilavasama*. As the function of "temple master" or "keeper of the temple keys" is taken care of by the officiating monk, there is no *gepaḷāna mahagamvasama*. The four pangus of the gamvasama are two *mīgondena* pangus (buffalo shares), which are the equivalents of the *mahagam* and the *mānagamvasama* of the devale, a *payinḍakiyana panguva*, which is,however, not a hereditary *(paravēni)* but a lease share *(māruvena panguva)*, and a *dura panguva*.

In the nilavasama three is a great concentration of service shares *(nila panguva)* in the narrow sense of the word, namely shares the tenants of wich have to cultivate the vihara muttettuva as rajakariya. In general the vihara pangus are not as specialized as the devale pangus, and are more "production oriented" than "ritual oriented." This is in line with a general difference between the two economic systems. The devalagama is completely geared to ritual functions, whereas the viharagama contains also many muttettuva fields which have to be worked by temple tenants solely for the economic support of the monastery and its monks. Most probably the greater power of the *vihārādhipati* has also influenced the pattern. The chief monk usually lived in the monastery just below the temple. His office was and is semi-hereditary in the sense that he himself could determine his successor and he had, consequently, enough time and a permanent interest to effect changes even against the resistance of others. Often the *vihārādhipati* or his designated successor performed the religious and supervisory functions which in the devale are connected with specific pangus. The *basnāyaka nilamē*, in contrast, lived far away; he was elected and appointed by an outside body for a limited period and he had to rely on local officers to maintain the temple system. Some differences between the structure of the viharagam and that of the devalagam can be explained by the different roles and "job descriptions" of the religious specialists. The kapurala was a peasant and could own and work a share of the temple land himself. The bhikkhu, however, was bound by the rules of his order and by Sinhalese Buddhist customs not to engage in agricultural pursuits. He could, consequently, not own a service share, so that we have only four instead of five temple officers' shares *(gamvasama)*.

The *basic* structure of the vihara estate and the devale estate is thus similar, though there are some significant variations. The dual organization of the temple is, consequently, evident also in the land tenure system. The third organizational complex which we found to be important for the explanation of ritual, the royal complex, is represented by similarly organized estates, the *gabadagam* (royal lands) and the *nindagam* (lands of lords).[1] The latter are hereditary lands for which services *(rājakāriya)* are due to Kandyan aristocratic families *(radala)*. The nindagam system, which I will not analyze here, was officially abolished in 1970 on the recommendations of the Commission on Tenure of Lands of Viharagam, Devalagam and Nindagam, of 1955 (SPI, 1956). We shall now have a closer look at the services which the temple tenants must perform.

3. Temple Service (Rajakariya)

The services the tenants of the devalagama are expected to perform can be grouped into five types:

(a) The cultivation of the devale muttettuva and related activities. The muttettus form the major part of the bandara lands, described above. There is no direct religious or ritual significance attached to these services except those commonly connected with paddy agriculture, like reaping the first sheaf of paddy at an auspicious hour.

(b) Repairs and maintenance of the temple. Most of these services have to be performed only when the occasion arises, like felling timber to be

1 Gabadagam and nindagam are closely related and both belong to the palace system. "Villages and fields attached to a *gabadāva* were frequently granted to chiefs as perequisites of office, or to individuals as rewards, and *gabadagam* so granted were known as *nindagam*. If a grant was made in perpetuity, it was designated *pravēni nindagam*" (Pieris 1956: 50). "Most, if not all, *nindagam* were bestowed as perquisites of office, and could be resumed by the Crown." (Pieris 1956: 60).

used for repairing the temple or supplying straw and thatching the roofs of the various subsidiary buildings. There are also a number of supplies to be used during rituals and temple festicals, which temple tenants have to furnish. Illumination of the temple is apparently regarded as important and various supplies, like wicks, rags and oil, are expressly mentioned in the service tenure register.

(c) Services and supplies for temple officials. There are a variety of services which emphasize and ritualize the relationship between tenants and the templelord and his officials. To appear before a landlord on Sinhalese New Year with forty leaves of betel is a standard practice in Ceylon.

The three types of rajakariya mentioned so far have little to do with the religious function of the devale. They are more or less the same services villagers had to perform for the king or for aristocratic officials of the Kandyan Kingsom. The following two types are directly related to the religious activities of the temple.

(d) Participation in the daily and weekly rituals. (These are the services we have already described at some length in our analysis of temple ritual in Chapter IV).

(e) Services for temple festivals. Most of them have to be performed before and during the annual perahära and include preparatory jobs, like decorating the temple and fetching elephants, walking in the procession as temple official, musician or flag bearer, and ritual activities like making offering to the gods.

Table 20 lists all types of services to be performed by devale tenants. It should be noted, however, that these services differ considerably in importance and effort as well as in the number of tenants who have to perform the respective duty.

Table 20

Services (Rājakāriya) Due to Lankātilaka Devālaya

A. Cultivation of Templeland (Muttettuva) and Related Activities

1. To supervise cultivation of muttettuva
2. To cultivate muttettuva
3. To measure paddy issued from the granary
4. To prepare seedpaddy for sowing
5. To sow paddy in muttettuva
6. To reap first sheaf of paddy at auspicious hour
7. To reap paddy
8. To lend buffaloes for thrashing
9. To take part in threshing
10. To carry paddy to granary
11. To watch granary or temple

B. Repairs and Maintenance of Temple

1. To supervise nilakāraya working for temple

2. To weed the temple compound
3. To weed near ānamessara
4. To help repairing temple
5. To supply tools to fell timber
6. To fell timber
7. To supply pattika planks
8. To supply clay and firewood to bake tiles
9. To wash the temple
10. To whitewash the temple
11. To thatch the granary and the lower temple
12. To thatch the temple kitchen
13. To supply straw
14. To supply oil
15. To supply valankat (pingo pots) to temple
16. To supply thread for randōli
17. To supply rags for torches
18. To supply wicks for oil lamps
19. To supply clothing to temple officers
20. To lend clothing to people fetching vattoruva
21. To supply two mats

C. Services and Supplies for Temple Officials

1. To appear before officials with 40 betel leaves
2. To give vegetables and pehidum to officials
3. To give sweetmeats to officials
4. To give provisions (adukkuva) and lodgings to officials
5. To build a toilet (diyagē) for the basnāyaka nilamē
6. To wait on the basnāyaka nilamē during Kandy perahära
7. To give pots to officials
8. To carry gifts (penumkat) to the basnāyaka nilamē
9. To work for the basnāyaka nilamē
10. To give 40 betel leaves to the vaṇṇakurāla
11. To give two meals of rice to pannikayā
12. To carry baggage of messengers (payindakāraya) to Kandy

D. Participation in Weekly Ritual

1. To open the temple doors
2. To make offerings (pūjāva)
3. To cook offerings (multän)
4. To light lamps
9. To supply oil for nānumura ritual
6. To boil lime for nānumura ritual
7. To supply and prepare sandalwoodpaste for tēvāva
8. To blow the conch shell (hakgeḍiya)
9. To play the kettle drum (tammätan)
10. To blow the oboe (horanäva)
11. To play the drum (davula)
12. To dance on Saturdays
13. To daub the temple floor with cowdung
14. To daub the kitchen floor with cowdung

E. Services for Temple Festivals

1. To erect triumphal arches
2. To erect ānamesara
3. To lend a talipot branch muttuva for the procession

4. To fetch elephants for the procession
5. To dig a pond for water to wash the elephants
6. To supply an arecanut tree for an arch
7. To decorate the temple
8. To fetch the list of orders for the festivals
9. To be at the dēvāle during the perahära
10. To attend the Kandy perahära
11. To go to the river for the watercutting ceremony
12. To go to Gurudeniya for the New-rice-festival
13. To take account of offerings
14. To be present when the treasureroom is opened
15. To attend the festivals and go in the procession
16. To carry the weapons of the gods (ranayudha) in the procession
17. To carry the palanquin (randōli) in the procession
18. To carry pearl umbrellas in the procession(mutukuḍē)
19. To carry shields (paliha) in the procession
20. To carry palmyra umbrellas (vadanatalatta) in procession
21. To carry flags (koḍiya) in the procession
22. To play the kettle drum (tammätan)
23. To blow the oboe (horanāva)
24. To play the drum (davula)
25. To dance in the procession
26. To sing at the throne house (sinhāsanäya)
27. To make offerings
28. To light lamps
29. To perform alatti (offering of lights)
30. To chant pirit

Table 21

Percentage Distribution of Types of Rājakāriya by Group of Pangu and Caste, Lankātilaka Dēvālaya

*Pangu No.**	*Caste*	*Type of Rājakāriya*									
		A Cultivation of Muttettu		*B Repairs and Maintenance*		*C Services to Officials*		*D Weekly Ritual*		*E Temple Festivals*	
		%	*(Units)*	*%*	*(Units)*	*%*	*(Units)*	*%*	*(Units)*	*%*	*(Units)*
1–5	Goyigama	16	(18)	37	(41)	16	(18)	2	(2)	28	(31)
6–9	Goyigama	15	(7)	25	(12)	13	(6)	15	(7)	32	(15)
10–13	Goyigama	19	(4)	38	(8)	14	(3)	0	(—)	29	(6)
14–15	Badahäla, Hēna	0	(—)	55	(6)	18	(2)	0	(—)	27	(3)
16–19	Beravāyā	14	(9)	43	(28)	18	(12)	6	(4)	18	(12)
20–22	Padu	18	(4)	27	(6)	18	(4)	5	(1)	32	(7)
23	(Buddhist monk)	0	(—)	0	(—)	0	(—)	0	(—)	100	(1)
1–23	All Castes	15	(42)	37	(101)	16	(45)	5	(14)	27	(75)

* For names of pangus see Table 18.

As I have already mentioned the services are connected with shares of temple land *(panguva)*. The tenants of one particular panguva have to perform all the services attached to it. Traditionally the services attached to each panguva can only be performed by members of a particular caste (see Table 18). One might therefore jump to the conclusion that each type of service is connected with only one particular panguva or at least with only one group of pangus, owned by members of the same caste. This is, however, not the case. As table 21 shows, the five types of services are distributed almost equally among the groups of pangus. This means that all castes participate more or less equally in the same type of activities. The condition that certain pangus can only be held by members of a particular caste arises because each panguva tends to have at least *one* caste-specific service attached to it. This service normally gives its name to the panguva. Thus tenants of the *hēvisi* or *tammätan panguva* (kettledrum share, number 17 in Table 18) have to beat the kettledrum at the weekly rituals and at temple festivals, a service which can only be performed by members of the drummer's caste *(beravāyā)*. In addition to this service the tenants of the *tammätan panguva* also have to cultivate five las of the devale muttettuva (A 2 in Table 20), to take part in the threshing of devale paddy (A 9), to carry paddy to the granary (A 10) and to watch the temple at night for three months per year (A 11). Furthermore there are services connected with the maintenance of the temple, like weeding the temple compound four times a year (B 2) or whitewashing the temple (B 10), services directly to the temple lord (C 9) and preparations for the temple festival (E 2). All these services are performed together with members of other castes and tenants of other pangus.

Work and ritual is thus organized on a *multicaste basis*, and one is tempted to adopt the usual functionalist "explanation" of the "integrative function of ritual." The work or ritual activities themselves certainly integrate the participants at least to a certain extent, as otherwise both work and ritual could not successfully be performed. Whether this temporary integration leads, however, to an integration of the village society is doubtful or at least difficult to prove. A more sensible explanation of the multi-caste basis of work and ritual is that a structure of authority is built into work and ritual by joining different castes.

As members of all castes have, for instance, to "weed the temple compound" the work groups are automatically structured hierarchically: members of the highest caste will, on account of their caste status, supervise the work of the lower castes which will again differentiate the various parts of the work, like weeding and removing the garbage, according to their caste status. The system is thus designed to work with a minimum of formal supervision through one of the temple officials. In a somewhat modified Durkheimian terminology it means that a good part of the organization of work is achieved through "mechanical solidarity" whereas only some aspects have to be "organically" specified through rules and regulations laid down in the service tenure register.

The list of the services to be performed for the vihara is more or less the same.

I will therefore not repeat it here. The major difference between devale and vihara services is that the latter has a higher percentage of service units devoted to the cultivation of muttettus, a fact already discussed in the last section.

4. Temple Villages

Most of the temple tenants live in four villages in the immediate vicinity of Lankatilaka Temple. These villages are Hiyarapitiya where the temple itself is situated, the devale village of Hiddaulla to the West, and the two vihara villages of Arawwawala and Rabbegamuva[1] to the South and North of the temple. The village of Arawwawala was formerly a nindagam village which became viharagam in the late 19th century. The centre of each village is not a village green, a road or a temple, but rather a fairly long and narrow paddy field stretching along the bottom of a valley and ascending in terraces towards its forked ends. The village houses and huts are clustered on the slopes of the mountains, hidden in the lush tropical green of their village gardens, into which narrow footpaths extend like tunnels. Between and above the gardens start small plantations of tea, rubber, coconuts and spices. The higher hilltops, especially West of Hiddaulla, are covered with tropical rain forest. (See Table 22). The population

Table 22

Land Utilization of Temple Villages, 1964

	Hiyarapitiya		*Arawwawala*		*Rabbegamuva*		*Hiddaulla*	
	acres	*p.c.*	*acres*	*p.c.*	*acres*	*p.c.*	*acres*	*p.c.*
Paddy	43	26.2	47	30.1	50	31.8	82	27.9
Other food crops	11	6.7	11	7.1	4	2.5	6	2.0
Tea	61	37.2	46	29.5	15	9.6	164	55.8
Rubber	—	—	8	5.1	—	—	4	1.4
Coconut	4	2.4	4	2.6	—	—	38	12.9
Other comm. crops	38	23.2	34	21.8	88	56.1	—	—
Forest etc.	7	4.3	6	3.8	—	—	—	—
	164	100.0	156	100.0	157	100.0	294	100.0
Agricultural Lands								
Paddy land *(Kumbura)*	43	27.4	47	29.4	50	31.8	82	27.9
Gardens *(vatta)*	11	7.0	11	6.9	4	2.5	6	2.0
Highlands	103	65.6	102	63.7	103	65.6	206	70.1
	157	100.0	160	100.0	157	99.9	294	100.0

Source: Unpublished records, Statistical Office, Kandy.

1 See Sievers 1964 for a short geographical description of Rabbegamuva.

has roughly tripled since the turn of the century (see Table 23), whereas the agricultural lands have hardly been extended at all. Though yields have gone up, more cash crops have been planted and additional employment has been found on nearby tea estates or in the town of Kandy and Gampola (See Table 24), the wealth and living standard of the ordinary villager has certainly declined considerably.[1] Only the landlords, including the temple lords of Lankatilaka, have profited from higher yields on constant or expanding acreages. It is not

Table 23

Population Growth of Temple Villages, 1881–1964

Village	*Number of Residents*							
	1880	*1891*	*1901*	*1911*	*1921*	*1931*	*1953*	*1964*
Hiyarapitiya	228	186	223	255	254	335	417	539
Arawwawala	176	176	199	234	237	307	469	628
Rabbegamuva	242	207	248	298	310	453	626	831
Hiddaulla	266	261	326	399	405	627	697	888
Central Province in 1,000	474	475	623	672	718	953	1,367	

Sources: Census of Ceylon 1881–1953, Fieldnotes, information received from the Statistical Office, Kandy; and List of rice-ration books issued in 1964, Grama Sävakas' Offices, and Office of the D.R.O. for Udunuvara and Yatinuvara.

Table 24

Gainfully Employed Population of Temple Villages, 1964

	Hiyarapitiya		*Arawwawala*		*Rabbegamuva*		*Hiddaulla*	
	No.	*p.c.*	*No.*	*p.c.*	*No.*	*p.c.*	*No.*	*p.c.*
Farmers	31	(33)	24	(22)	109	(46)	116	(34)
Plantation Labourer	1	(1)	2	(2)	90	(38)	152	(45)
Casual Labourer	47	(49)	42	(38)	25	(10)	43	(13)
Handloom textile worker	—	—	—	—	6	(2)	11	(3)
Carpenter	—	—	3	(3)	2	(1)	2	(1)
Mason	2	(2)	2	(2)	—	—	2	(1)
Brick and tile worker	2	(2)	6	(5)	2	(1)	—	—
Blacksmith	—	—	—	—	—		2	(1)
Wholesale and retail trader	10	(11)	30	(27)	4	(2)	12	(3)
Others	2	(2)	1	(1)	—	—	—	
Total gainfully employed	95	(100)	110	(100)	238	(100)	340	(101)

Source: Unpublished records, Statistical Office, Kandy.

1 For details on the deppressed state of peasants in Central Ceylon see the Kandyan Peasantry Report, S.P. 1951.

so much the problem of landlessness—less than one-third of all families own no land—but extreme land fragmentation through equal inheritance rights of siblings, which creates economic distress. Assuming that an average family needs at least one acre of paddy land and some additional plot of village garden to subsist, the fact that 53 per cent of all families in Hiyarapitiya, 58 per cent in Arawwawala, 68 per cent in Hiddaulla and 76 per cent in Rabbegamuva own less than one-half acre of land or no land at all becomes significant and sheds some light on the economic pressures to which villagers are subjugated (see Table 25). Extreme competition and struggle for additional land has thus

Table 25
Land Ownership in Temple Villages, 1961–62

	Number of Families							
	Hiyarapitiya		*Arawwawala*		*Rabbegamuva*		*Hiddaulla*	
	No.	*p.c.*	*No.*	*p.c.*	*No.*	*p.c.*	*No.*	*p.c.*
No. of families	107	(100)	99	(99)	144	(100)	155	(100)
Owning no land	28	(26)	29	(29)	48	(33)	17	(11)
Owning less than ½ acre	29	(27)	28	(28)	62	(43)	88	(57)
Owning over ½ and less than 3 acres	41	(38)	32	(32)	21	(15)	38	(24)
Owning over 3 and less than 5 acres	2	(2)	6	(6)	9	(6)	12	(8)
Owning 5 acres and more	7	(7)	4	(4)	4	(3)	—	—
Tenancy of paddy Lands, no of parcels	78	(100)	98	(100)	116	(100)	150	(99)
Owner cultivated	23	(29)	52	(53)	56	(48)	80	(53)
Tenant cultivated *(andē)*	55	(71)	35	(36)	53	(46)	56	(37)
Cultivated by lessees	—		3	(3)	7	(6)	14	(9)
Cultivated in rotatation (tattumaru)	—		8	(8)	—		—	

Source: Unpublished records, Statistical Office, Kandy.

increased the power of the temple lords and at the same time made their social position rather precarious. Discontent with the existing temple tenure system is widespread and the temple lords, both the chief Buddhist monk as well as the Basnayaka Nilame of the devale, are openly criticized. In systematic interviews with all temple tenants in one of the temple villages, only few gave religious reasons, like earning religious merit, for complying with their duties as temple servants. Most peasants objected to performance of rajakariya, but stated that they had to obey for fear of eviction from their land or other economic deprivations.[1]

1 The legal provision to commute temple services against a small yearly payment was generally not known by villagers.

The basic social structure of the temple villages is determined by caste and kinship. As became already apparent in our discussion of the religious organization of Lankatilaka, concern with purity and pollution makes it necessary to employ members of different castes for ritual tasks and other temple services. The temple villages are consequently multi-caste villages, which makes their social structure rather complex and somewhat different from most other Kandyan villages described in the social science literature (Leach 1961, Yalman 1967, Tambiah 1965, Obeyesekere 1967, Robinson 1968b).

The majority of all Kandyan Sinhalese are Goyigama, i.e. members of the highest caste. The village of Hiyarapitiya in which the temple, but only a fraction of the temple land, is situated, conforms largely to this pattern as almost two-thirds of all families are Goyigama. The temple villages proper, in which most of the viharagam and devalagam is found and where most temple tenants live, have only a few high caste families (see Table 26). Villagers in the area are very aware of this fact and their evaluation of the status of these villages is derived from the number of Goyigama families resident in the villages. Thus outsiders as well as Goyigamas agree on the following rank order: 1. Hiyarapitiya, 2. Hiddaulla, 3. Arawwawala, 4. Rabbegamuva. It is important to note that it is not, as one might expect, the affiliation with the Buddhist vihara, nor

Table 26
Caste Structure of Temple Villages, 1964

Castes	*Number of House holds*			
	Hiyarapitiya	*Arawwawala*	*Rabbegamuva*	*Hidaulla*
Goyigama (Farmers)	69	15	2	35
Karāva (Fishermen)	1	1	—	—
Navandanna (Smiths)	—	—	9	11
Hunu (Lime Burners)	5	—	—	13
Rada or Hēna (Washermen)	9	—	—	5
Badahäla (Potters)	—	—	—	12
Beravā (Tom-tom Beaters)	10	15	—	29
Durāva or Padu (Servants)	10	22	—	24
Batgam or Padu (Servants)	2	11	—	18
Batgam-Durayi (Servants, Warriors)	—	1	111	—
(Muslim)	—	28	—	1
(No information)	1	9	6	—
	107	102	128	148
Summery (Muslim and n.i. excluded)	p.c.	p.c.	p.c.	p.c.
High caste (Goyigama)	65	23	2	24
Service castes	34	77	98	76
	100	100	100	100

Source: fieldnotes 1964–66.

historical connections with important aristocratic families, but caste that is the major factor in determining the social status of a village or a hamlet within a village. In keeping with this evaluation is the attitude towards rajakariya for the vihara, as discussed above. Temple service is, in contrast to voluntary work or donations, *not* seen as religiously meritorious. A person does not gain merit *(pin)* and improve his karma by performance of temple service (rājakāriya).

In Table 26 the castes are arranged according to their hierarchical status position as it is normally recognized by Kandyan Sinhalese. However, the relative status of the last four castes mentioned, which account for the majority of the population in the three vihara and devale villages is disputed. The tom-tom beaters *(berevā)* are a well-known Sinhalese caste with a specific ritual and professional function, namely drumming at temples and at public festivals. The confusion is created by the three Batgam-Padu castes. They are not only strictly endogamous but also keep themselves socially apart, avoid contact with each other and each claim a higher status then the two other castes. They belong apparently to a whole group of Kandyan service castes without specific ritual or professional function. In the Kandyan political organization before British times they did not belong to a separate service-department *(badda)* as did most other service castes. (Pieris 1956: 186–7). Davy (1921: 127–8) reports that the paduvas "had to perform a variety of low services, as to build walls, and to thatch the roofs of houses, carry loads, bring wood and ornaments for arches, bear jingals in processions etc." These services correspond actually, by and large, to the temple services they have to perform today for Lankatilaka. Why they are in conflict and separation is difficult to ascertain. Differences in names do not amount to much. Other villagers were often confused in their terminology (which normally does not happen with them in such an important matter as caste) and the terms used are often "polite" forms applied to other castes of the same group as well. So "*batgama*" (lit. rice village) was an alternative term for a particular type of royal service village "usually inhabited by people of low caste liable to public services" (Codrington 1938: 24–25), and *durāva*, not to be confused with the toddy-tapper caste of the Ceylonese low country, and *durayi* are honorific terms for low caste people or their chiefs. (Ryan 1953: 122). On the whole, "caste" was a rather explosive topic to discuss in the temple villages, except perhaps with high status Goyigama villagers. The system, especially in the lower echelons, seems to be fairly flexible and dynamic.[1]

1 Ryan's (1953) discussion of these castes is not very clear and Yalman (1967) has focussed on other problems. Robinson (1968b: 421) has called attention "to the necessity of understanding the range of variation possible within the kinship structure of a single social system and cultural area" (Kandyan Sinhalese). The same probably applies to caste as well. The regional variability of Sinhalese social structure has probably mislead Ryan and Straus to compare Sinhalese with Thai society and call it "loosely structured" (Ryan and Straus 1954; Straus 1966). For a detailed discussion of the loose structure issue see Evers (1969b and 1968b).

Appendix to Chapter V

5. A Note on Sinhalese Measures of Land

The extent of land is not given in a surface measure but it the amount of rice used to sow a plot of land. The actual size of land sown by one *amuṇa or päḷa* of seed paddy consequently varies considerably according to fertility, irrigation and position of the land. In the Kandy district one acre of irrigated paddy fields *(kumbura)* is sown with approximately two *päl* of seed paddy. In the case of highlands, like gardens *(vatta)* or chena *(hēn)* the extent varies considerably.

Sinhalese Measure of Land

1 *yāḷa* = 12 *amuṇa*
1 *amuṇa* = 4 *pāḷa*
1 *pāḷa* = 10 *las (kuruṇi)*
Abbreviated: a-p-l.
(amuna, pl. *amunu; päḷa*, pl. *päl; lāha*, pl. *lās; kuruṇiya*, pl. *kuruṇi)*

Approximate Acre-Equivalent of One Amuna in Various Districts

District	*(1) Paddy Fields*	*(2) High-lands*	*Source*
Kandy	2 acres	2 acres	(1) Field notes (2) SP I 1956: 29
Kegalle		5 acres	(2) SP I 1956: 29
Kurunegala		40 acres	(2) SP I 1956: 29
Anuradhapura	4 acres(?)	40 acres	(1) Leach 1961: 182 (2) SP I 1956: 29
Galle (Himdum Pattu)	5.6 acres	n.i.	(1) Obeycsekere 1967: 7

CHAPTER SIX

Perspective on Theravada Buddhism: The Social Organization of Contrasting Values

1. The Basic Problem

THE social organization of Theravada Buddhism appears to be simple in theory. There is a body of ascetic monks, supported by a pious laity, leading an austere life geared to learning, preaching and meditation. A closer look shatters the appearance of simplicity. There are gods and demons, priests and monks, landlords and aristocrats, elaborate rituals and festivals. In the preceding study a good deal of effort was put into the task of simply describing the various parts of this social and cultural complex and understanding how the parts relate to each other. It was assumed throughout that there must be basic principles organizing the whole system and that these principles could be detected in this study of a central institution, the temple. The very fact that the temple and its surrounding social and religious structure have survived for more than six centuries makes this assumption plausible. In addition to the task of describing and analysing an important institution of a major religion for the first time, a more general problem emerges. This problems seems to be applicable to a large number of societies and can be posed as follows:
Sinhalese society has harboured throughout most of its history three constrasting religious value systems. There was Theravada Buddhism, emphasizing withdrawal from this world, individual salvation and the virtues of giving; there was the worship of Gods, emphasizing the perils of this world and their management; and then there was the allegiance to the divine king, stressing submission to supreme authority. Though these value systems were closely interrelated and overlapped in many instances, there was apparently never any doubt about the identity of each system. Basic differences between them were always recognised. The introduction of new religious value systems and their co-existence with older ones is certainly a very common phenomenon in world history. In most cases one of the following developments took place: Either one system submerged into the realm of folk religion and superstitions ("displacement"), or a merger and accommodation took place ("syncretism"), or the laity was split into adherents of either religion ("differentiation"). The latter occurred in Ceylon with the introduction of Islam and Christianity. The extraordinary fact, however, remains that neither with the introduction of Theravada Buddhism nor with

attempts to establish Hinduism did the laity split into adherents of either religion. It is equally remarkable that the elaborate ritual and cult of the god-king *(dēvāraja)* did not develop into a separate religion with its own followers. The development of Mahayana Buddhism in particular and Chinese and Japanese religion in general provide contrasting examples. Though here, also, the differentiation of the laity is not as clear-cut as perhaps between Hindus, Muslims and Christians in India, nevertheless sectarian movements, allegiance to one particular religious value system, development of distinct "state religions" like Shintoism, etc. resulted in social differentiation along religious lines. Not so in Sinhalese society. The peasant mass, though stratified into castes, remained culturally undifferentiated. Whatever *social* differentiation there was could not be related to the three contrasting religious value systems mentioned above. Even the South Indian Pattern, according to which the veneration of a particular deity is often associated with a particular caste or lineage, was unknown in Central Ceylon (Yalman 1964: 118, Gough 1960: 43, Dumont 1957). Differentiation took only place at the very top of the social and cultural system, namely into the three socio-religious systems discovered in our analysis of Lankatilaka temple: the vihara system, the devale system and the palace system.

The basic problem then can be formulated as follows: How is it possible to maintain a social system over a long period of time in which the majority of the population is culturally and religiously *undifferentiated* while at the same time contrasting religious value systems and their concomitant social organizations are perpetuated? How is it possible to have separate socio-religious structures, identifying and dramatizing separate values, without splitting and differentiating the members of a society in their allegiance to either system?[1]

2. The Social Organization of Contrasting Values

To attack this problem I shall introduce and explain some categories which will then be used to re-interpret the research findings and reformulate some basic hypotheses. It is perhaps important to note at this stage that we are here concerned with the overall organization of a complex society. The level of analysis is societal rather than local or individual. The following principles of social organization are to be distinguished for our analysis:

(a) *Parallelism*

In general terms parallelism is one of the basic organizational principles of any society. Many organizations or institutions in any society are structured similarly, repeat each other and have corresponding structural components. In 19th century Prussia one could speak of the army as "a state within the state"

1 Yalman (1965: 441) has expressed concern over this problem in a different context "...Can we speak of 'dual organization' when the society is not so divided, or when the social divisions are obscure, but where there is a symbolic system in which binary categories are prominent?". See also Ames 1964b and Evers 1965.

as both the government bureaucracy and the army were organized on strict principles of discipline and obedience, matched each other in power, and developed parallel institutions. A similar development took place in Indonesia recently. The army developed its own organizational structure parallel to the government bureaucracy. Both systems coexisted for quite some time until the army leadership took over the government itself in 1965. In a number of countries the army, navy and airforce are relatively independent "parallel organizations," competing with each other for power and influence.

The goals parallel organizations try to accomplish can be connected with quite different and contrasting value orientations. A socialist and a conservative party can be organized in the same way with an elected party leadership, committees, a "shadow cabinet" and a mass of supporting members, but their political goals and values might differ sharply. The organization of the mediæval church and the German empire was at times quite similar though at least some central values were quite different. The Buddhist Sangha in Thailand is organized parallel to the Thai government. The Thai King is matched by the Sangharaja ("King of the Sanhga"), the cabinet by a Sangha Council, etc. The goals and basic values of both organizations are, of course, not the same. It is nevertheless common that the mass of the population follows both contrasting value orientations. A Christian can sincerely recite the Ten Commandments in church or a Buddhist the five sil and a few moments later forget about the the pledge not to kill and cheer a returning brigade of his country's glorious army. Parallel organizations tend to limit the perception of the contrast between value systems by relating them to *specific* instances or structural elements ("oppositions"). The perception of organizational parallels becomes predominant.

If the value contrasts become generalized and all-pervading, parallel organization may extend through the society as a whole. This would lead to a structure known in Dutch society as "verzuiling" (columnization) and in Indonesian society as "aliran" (stream). In this case parallelism becomes the general principle of social organization. Contrasting value orientations (in Indonesia modernist and orthodox Islam, Javanese peasant and court values, in Holland Protestantism, Catholicism and a religious humanitarianism), create parallel organizations like political parties, religious organizations and schools. Extreme parallelism tends to become unstable, though the creation of parallel organizations is an attempt to regulate conflict, i.e. to turn open conflict into "competition" (see below). "Avoidance" between adherents of different value systems is made possible as parallel organizations diminish social contacts.[1] A special case of parallelism has been discussed by Lévy-Strauss and others under the term "dual organization". According to Lévy-Strauss (1969: 69), dual organization describes "a system in which the members of the community, whether it be a tribe or a village, are divided into two parts which maintain complex relationships varying from open hostility to very close intimacy, and

1 "Avoidance" is a well-known principle to diminish structural conflicts in tribal societies.

with which various forms of rivalry and co-operation are usually associated." Together with dual organization we often find a "dichotomy of power between a secular chief and a sacred chief, or a secular chief and a military chief." Lévy-Strauss relates dual organizations to a "fundamental structure of the human mind", the principle of reciprocity. I maintain that reciprocity between two contrasting factions is admittedly the most simple and perhaps therefore a very common arrangement, but other more complex forms are also found. Of importance is the notion that dual or parallel organization regulates conflict in a society. Lévy-Strauss relates this idea again to a fundamental structure of the human mind. He regards the notion of reciprocity "as the most immediate form of integrating the opposition between self and others."

(b) *Opposition* (supplementary opposition).

Differing cultural values can be stressed or dramatized by ritual acts, aspects of roles, structural features of an organization and symbols. If contrasting values are set against each other in pairs, triplets, etc., i.e. if they are seen as directly related but diametrically opposed, we will speak of "oppositions." There are of course many values and their related symbols, acts and social structures which are seen as different but totally unrelated. Thus a Christian confirmation and the election of a party official express quite different values and would not be seen as related or opposed in any way. Donning a fake uniform and wearing long hair as opposed to wearing a uniform of the U.S.Army and short hair could be seen as expressing opposed but related cultural values, which in this care, however, are not embedded in "parallel organization:" Hippie type organization and the organizational structure of the U.S.Army are quite different and far from parallel. Conflicts due to different values have been frequent between them. It is perhaps interesting to note that, in contrast, conflict between Army leadership and working class organizations has been minimal in recent American history. Both are part of "parallel organizations," armed forces and economic enterprises, with similar organizational structures.

"Oppositions" thus balance each other emphasizing related but contrasting values. They are therefore correlative and antagonistic at the same time, to borrow a phrase used by Lévy-Strauss (1969: 69–83) in another context. Oppositions *specify* essential differences between two or more values systems stressing at the same time the *equality* of the values expressed. As oppositions point to specific and limited value differences they make it possible that contrasting values are expressed by parallel organizations.

The combination of oppositions and parallel organizations allows, I would hypothesize, the maintenance of contrasting value systems acknowledged as such by a culturally undifferentiated mass of population. Different values, contained by specific, balanced and complementary oppositions, provide a chance to avoid splitting a society along value lines. Translated into the terminology of the sociology of religion this would mean that both syncretism and sect formation would be avoided, as in the case of Sinhalese society.

(c) *Competition and Hierarchization*

Parallel organizations tend to be in competition for resources, for the control over the mass of the population and for the dominance of their particular values. In other words, there is a tendency to turn complementary oppositions into hierarchical relations and parallel organizations into stratification systems. Hierarchization might succeed under certain conditions to a greater or lesser degree. In European history the prolonged struggle between crown and tiara, between Pope and Emperor, between Church and State resulted in the victory and predominance of the state; in Tibetan history Lamas were able to establish their Buddhist state and to dominate and partly replace Bon religion; in Ceylon the three parallel systems which I termed the vihara, the devale, and the palace systems had a varied history in which, by and large, the vihara system came to be acknowledged as the dominant one, though perhaps not as dominant as Buddhist historical sources want to portray it. A major problem inherent in the dynamics of these systems is that historical material are usually supplied by a minute minority of specialists from either system, each trying to prove the dominance of its own organization. As Ceylon history has been seen primarily as a Theravada Buddhist history and is definitely related as such in the major chronicles, the view of the peasant masses acknowledging the coexistence, and to a certain extent equality, of the three value systems has probably been underestimated. In any case, competition and hierarchization certainly took place, as I will discuss in due course.

To sum up: Max Weber has defined "competition" as regulated conflict. In our case the regulation took place through the principles of parallellism and opposition which have successfully maintained and balanced the social system of Sinhalese religion. "Parallelism" and "opposition" are defined as principles of social organization according to which differing, though closely related, value systems find expression in similarly structured social organizations ("parallel organizations") with certain specific features in which the differences in the values concerned are contrasted ("supplementary oppositions"). "Competition and hierarchization" refer to the dynamics of the systems.

3. The Vihara, Devale and Palace Systems Reconsidered

In the preceding chapters I have already alluded to parallelism and opposition in general terms. I shall now reconsider the data presented in more specific terms, using the concepts outlined above.

The parallelism in the structure of the vihara, devale and palace systems is striking indeed. The most "unusual" building complexes in rural and premodern urban Ceylon were the Buddhist temple and monastery *(vihāraya)*, the temple for the gods *(dēvālaya)* and either the manor *(valavva)*, or in the capital, the royal palace *(maḷigāva)* (Figure 10). There were also the three corresponding

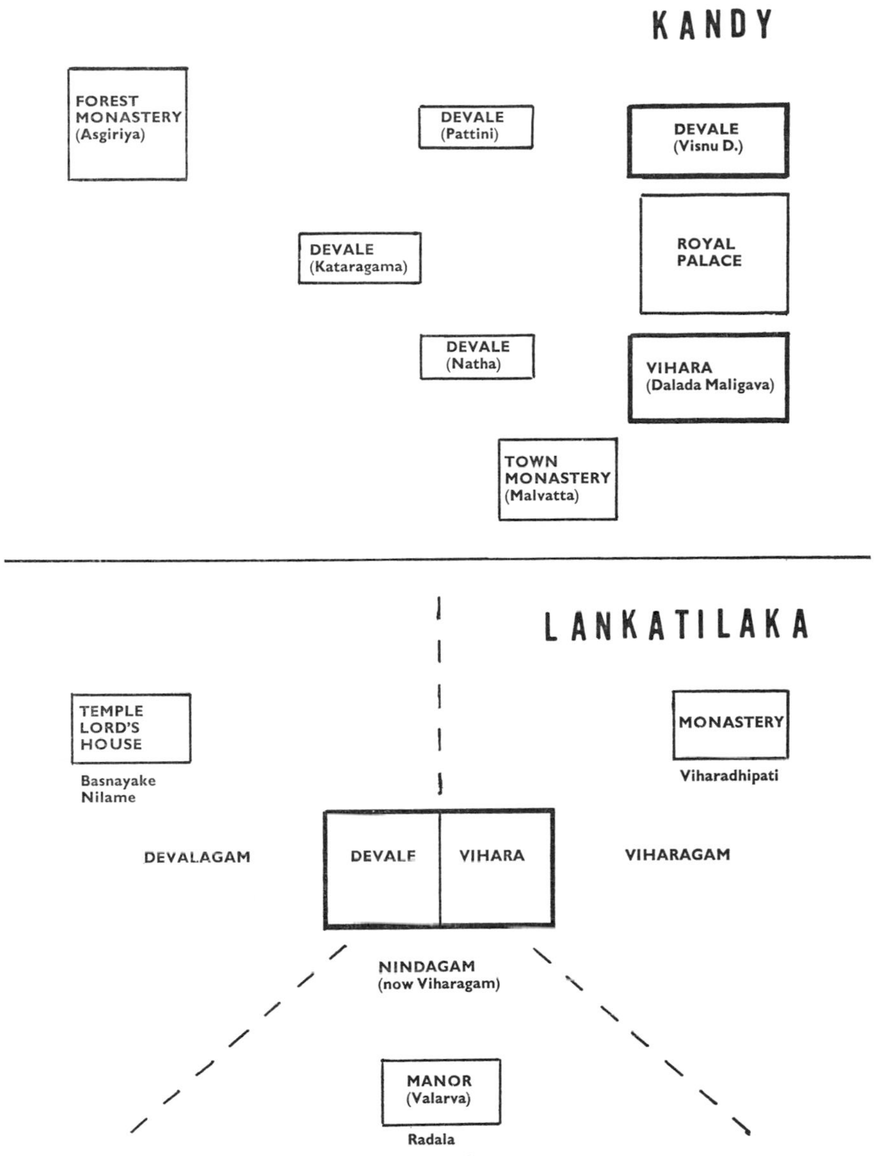

Fig. 10

Diagram of the Vihara, Devale and Palace Systems in Kandy and at Lankatilaka

landed estates, the *vihāragam*, *dēvālagam* and *nindagam* or *gabādagam*.[1] All three building complexes were places of worship. The Buddha image, the image of the God and the King were approached with different intentions but in the same way. The social structure of the three systems followed the same orga-

1 The differences between valavva and maligava and between nindagam and gabadagam will be discussed below.

nizational principles and there are corresponding religious specialists, landlords and administrative officials. Table 27 depicts this parallel organization and refers to the respective chapters in which details are given.

I now turn to the "oppositions" based on contrasting religious values. One of the central contrasts is described by the terms *lōkōttara* (otherworldly, relating to the next world) and *laukika* (pertaining to this world, mundane, worldly). The first refers to Buddhist activities and beliefs, the second to the worship of the gods. This distinction has been related by many observers from early Ceylon visitors to modern social anthropologists. Robert Knox commented in 1681 (p. 115–117) that "there are many both Gods and Devils, which they (the Sinhalese) worship... Those, whom they call Dio or Gods... belong the Government on earth, and of all things appertaining to this life... There is another great God, whom they call Buddon, unto whom the Salvation of Souls belongs." A learned Sinhalese, Dandris de Silva Gooneratne, reported in 1865 (cited in Yalman 1964: 138) that "Buddhism does not hold out worldly advantages or immediate rewards in this life... Its task is to obtain salvation for the soul...a consummation to be attained only in another state of existence... Demonism on the other hand deals with the concerns of this life and of this life alone." (Gooneratne 1865: 5 ff). Modern studies on Sinhalese religion confirm this connotation. "The primary division in Sinhalese religion is...between *lōkōttara* and *laukika* value orientations...", says Ames (1964: 41).[1]

Table 27
Parallel Organization of Sinhalese Religion in Central Ceylon

Systems	*Religious Organization:*			*Social Organization:*	*Economic Organization:*
Building Complexes	*Supernatural Power*	*Religious Specialists*	*Ritual*	*Administrative Authority*	*Land and Services*
Vihāra	the Buddha	Bhikkhu (monk)	Buddha Pūjāva, Tēvāva	Vihārādhipati (Chief Monk)	Vihāragam (Monastic land and Services)
Dēvāle	the Gods	Kapurāla (priest)	Deva Pūjāva, Tēvāva	Basnāyaka Nilamē (Temple Lord)	Dēvālagam (Temple land and services)
Valavva Palace	the King	Brahmin (royal priest)	Tēvāva	Radala (Aristocratic Landlord)	Nindagam (Land of Lords and Services)

1 The contrast between lokuttara and laukika is therefore not related to the contrast between Buddha and Mara. See Windisch 1895 for an early discussion on this point. Dumont's (1962: 47–77) discussion on the opposition between *brahman* and *Kśatra* suggests that the *laukika-lōkōttara* opposition could be traced back far into Indian cultural history. He notes, "the separation within the religious universe of a shere or realm which

The terms lokuttara and laukika are connected with a host of contrasting values. One stresses withdrawal from the activities of this world, the other active involvement; one stresses giving without hope for rewards, the other exchange or bribes; one demands humility in this life, the other power and wealth; one demands abstention from sensual and sexual pleasures, the other sex and fertility. All these are, of course, contrasting values that are relevant to most religions, with the important difference, however, that in Sinhalese religion the contrasting systems are not defined as good and bad, sinful and virtuous.

In fact, a simple bifurcation of the world into the damned and the saved is prevented by the logic of karmic law, an altogether different principle. The status of all beings is determined by the amount of merit and demerit accumulated in former lives which places them on a continuum farther away or closer to nirvana. Eternal damnation is impossible.

The Buddha on the one hand and the gods on the other are thus clearly linked with these two contrasting value orientations. The king's position in this scheme is very interesting. The term *lōkōttara* also designates a king or sovereign (Clough 1892: 554), perhaps alluding to the component *uttara* (pre-eminent), but the common meaning of the term, "otherworldly", is certainly not lost. In practise the king was of course involved in the affairs of this world, i.e. his actions are *laukika*. In other respects the role of the king was also ambivalent. He was sometimes called a god, at other times a Boddhisattva[1] or, at least in Burma, even a Buddha (Sarkisyanz 1965). Villagers tended to solve this ambivalence by pointing out that the king used to be interested primarily in Buddhism and therefore built viharas and endowed them with land whereas the Queen was responsible for the construction of devales. This opinion is not based on historical facts but appears to express the female fertility connotations of the laukika devale system. On the other hand fertility rites have been traditionally associated with kingship in Ceylon as is evidenced by notes on royal rainmaking ceremonies found in the chronicles. The king could thus be seen as a mediator between *laukika* and *lōkōttara*, between the Buddha and the gods and eventually between cosmos and world.[2]

The basic opposition is expressed in the roles of the Buddhist monk *(bhikkhu)*, the priest *(kapurāḷa)* and the royal Brahmin *(purohita)*. Though their existence was part of the parallel structure, and their ritual acts, at least in the state temples and the palace, were functionally equivalent, important role aspects are nevertheless oppositions.

---

is opposed to the religious, and roughly corresponds to what we call political. As opposed to the realm of values and norms is the realm of force. As opposed to the *dharma* or universal order of the Brahman, is the realm of interest or advantage, *artha*." (Dumont 1962: 55).

1 The tradition that the king is a Bodhisattva goes back to at least the 10th century A.C. See the Jetavanarama Slab Inscription No. 2, E.Z.I: 240.

2 The analysis offered here would also explain the connection between the two aspects of Indian kingship, the magico-religious and the secular ones. It has apparently bothered indologists a good deal how to reconcile the respective political theories, the deva-raja cult and the "contract theory" of kingship as expounded in the Digha Nikaya or the Arthasastra.

The monk is celibate, and he has to shave his head and leave it uncovered while performing his ritual functions. His role is, at least symbolically, useless for everyday life as it is cut into small pieces and sewn together again. The kapurala, in contrast wears his hair long and covers his head during rituals. He has to be married, wears an ordinary though purified dress, or on special occasions a colourful uniform. All this symbolizes the contrast between laukika and lokkottara, between fertility and death, between concern with this world and the next.

The role of the royal Brahmin is difficult to analyse as it no longer exists. It seems that royal court Brahmins dropped out of the system altogether in early Kandyan times.[1] The respective office has aparently been taken over by the Diyavadana Nilame, the temple lord of the Temple of the Tooth[2] and by certain chief monks. This is indicated by the title "royal teacher" *(raja guru)* which the viharadhipati of Lankatilaka is still proud to bear.[3]

There are a number of other minor oppositions which I have mentioned in previous chapters, but parallelism is the overrriding organizational priciple. The systems as such are set against each other but their internal structures are similar. Oppositions are well balanced, clearly defined and limited to role aspects of the three heads of the three systems, the Buddha, the gods and the king, and to their immediate religious specialists.

The internal consistency of the system is extraordinary indeed and explains the stability over time. Though changes have, of course, occurred they seem to have taken the form of adjustments within a cybernatic system rather then revolutionary breaks with the past. Neither Buddhism nor the cult of the Gods has disappeared. The most radical changes were political ones, and especially the abolition of an indigenous government and king by the British in 1815 has severely challenged the durability of the religious system. It is, however, important to note that in the perception of Sinhalese villagers in Central Ceylon, the system has maintained a good deal of its original consistency. The palace system is vividly remembered and references to "the times of the kings" are made frequently. On the local level the Kandyan aristocracy, controlling temples and temple lands as basnayaka nilames or viharadhipatis or demanding rents and services for their nindagam lands, still represents the third system. And last, but not least, the resurgence of Sinhalese nationalism after independence forced politicians more and more into roles consistent with the traditional political system. The Governor is inaugurated in the Dalada Maligava in Kandy with a ritual that resembles the crowning ritual, prime ministers consult priests in devales before making important political decisions and take a keen interest, at least publicly, in affairs of the Sangha.

1 During the Gampola period land was still granted to Brahmins, though their function is not clear. See Miller, Ancient Inscriptions of Ceylon, No. 172, copperplate, probably of the time of Vijaya Bahu VI (1398–1409), confirming grant of a paddy field to to the Brahman Vendarasu Konda Perumal.

2 See Chapter IV: 4.

3 In Thailand this title is given to the chief Brahmin, the Phra Maha Rajakru.

Though a certain balance, I would say, has been maintained between the vihara, devale and palace systems throughout Sinhalese history, hierarchization and competition have tended to change the relevant power position of each system. In the preceding analysis I have stressed the equality and the parallelism of the systems, seen largely through the eyes of the monks, priests and peasants of Lankatilaka temple. From a different perspective, say either from a remote village (Obeysekere 1966) or from the national capital of Colombo, the relative importance and relevance of each system might be judged differently. By and large there is, and probably seldom has been, any doubt about the supremacy of the vihara system versus the devale system. Even at Lankatilaka the hierarchical distinctions were maintained. The Buddha occupied the centre of the temple, the vihara ritual took place before the devale ritual, and the prestige and deference accorded to the monks was greater than that accorded to the priests. Though in general the supremacy of the vihara system has been maintained on the national level, the general tendency during the present century has been a relatively growing importance of the devale system. The extraordinary growth of the cult of God Kataragama, both at a devale of that name in Southern Ceylon and elsewhere, indicates this trend. Exorcism and sorcery, the subsystem of the devale system, also seem to have increased rapidly, the clients being drawn more and more from the urban middle classes.[1]

The obvious explanation for this phenomenon has to do with our distinction between *laukika* and *lōkōttara*. The devale system is connected with the problems of this world. The greater the insecurity of this world and its problems and the greater the aspirations to solve these problems here and now, the more one is likely to turn to the activities of the devale system which promises immediate redress.

The vihara system has, of course, not remained uneffected by these developments. Here two trends have taken shape within the sphere of hierarchization and competition. One is consonant with the socio-religious structure as analysed in this study, the other is not. The latter is western-influenced Buddhist modernism which tries to prove that Theravada Buddhism is rationalistic, incorporates the basic ideas of modern science, and is therefore apt to solve the problems of a modernizing society. (Bechert 1966: 37ff). By its claim to be able to cope with and provide solutions for the problems of this world in this world, it is in direct competition with the aims and purview of the devale system. But rationalistic Buddhist modernism does not just seek to compete with the devale system. It is set outright to replace and destroy it as backward and superstitious. The other trend, originally associated with Buddhist modernism, is the "political Buddhism" of the 1950's. Its main battlecry was to restore Buddhism to its rightful place, which meant under the circumstances to give political power to the Buddhist monkhood. Its competition was directed against a particular government and its political system, not the devale system.

1 Personal communication from Gananath Obeysekere who is engaged in a long term study on sorcery in Ceylon. The growing importance of spirit shrines in another Buddhist country, Thailand, became apparent in a recent field study I conducted together with Arthur Stillman in Thailand.

APPENDIX

1. Sinhalese Rock-Inscription of 1344 A.C. at Lankatilaka Temple

THE construction of Lankatilaka Temple and the original landgrants made at that time are described in a Sinhalese and Tamil rock inscription. The characters are still clearly visible on the bare rock to the left of the main entrance of the vihara. These inscriptions were deciphered and translated, by Professor Paranavitana. The following text is taken, with minor changes, from his translation of the Sinhalese rock inscription (Paranavitana 1960a: 10–140).

"When One Thousand Two Hundred and Sixty-Six years had been completed in the era of the illustrious Śaka (king)—on the fifteenth of the bright half of Vesaga in the third year of me, named Bhuvanaikabāhu who has attained to the sovereignty at this time.

Whereas Senā-Laṁkā-adhikāra intimated to us that it would be desirable if there be an endowment for the maintenance in the future of this illustrious great monastery *(vihāra)* which was established on the summit of (the rock called) Panhalgala in Siṅguruvāṇa by the two venerable Communities of the eminent Saṅgha, which includes the great image-house established with the name of Śrī Laṁkātilaka consisting of the fourth storey complete with twenty-eight principal images and a thousand other images, the third storey which was caused to be constructed complete with Its Lordship the Principal Image and five other images, the second story which is completed with (the representations of) the twenty-eight Trees of Wisdom *(Bodhi)* and the twenty-four Predictions, caused to be constructed conjointly by all the chiefs *(mudali)* and the army, and the lowermost storey which is complete with images of Buddha and gods, to wit, Its Lordship the Principal Image seated on the Diamond Throne *(vajrāsana)* with back to Its Lordship the illustrious great Bodhitree, which (Image) has been made by having installed within it a relic-image containing two hundred and sixty-five Lordships of relics, with three thousand Lordships of painted images (including the images of) the Lord Maitrī Bodhisattva, Lord Lokeśvara Nātha, the forms of the divinities beginning with Suyāma, Santuṣita, Śakra, Brahma, Viṣṇu and Maheśvara, the images of the divine consorts of all these aforesaid personages, the images of the Lord, the divine king Kihireli Upulvan, who has taken (upon himself) the protection of Laṁkā, and the divine kings Sumana, Vibhīṣaṇa, Gaṇapati, Kandakumāra and others and their consorts—which (storey) was caused to be constructed by this personage himself, namely Senā-Laṁkā-adhikāra, and which (image-house) was caused to be constructed by us, our chiefs *(mudali)* and the host together, having spent thirty-six millions in *masuran* reckoning on account of things including paddy, gold, silver and cloths given to many artisans including Sthapatirāyara, from the time the base-moulding *(välikonda)* was started up to the completion of the finial of this image-house—which *(vihāra)* includes the image of solid bronze, installed in the pavilion measuring twenty-eight cubits, which was caused to be constructed by Senā-Laṁkā-adhikāra through his sons and the ladies of his household, the two convents for monks established so that their lordships the members of the great communities of the two fraternities, including the elders of moderate wants, may rest there with comfort and which comprises flower gardens and orchards of fruit trees—(as it was so intimated, we have ordered) in this wise.

An extent of field sufficient for the sowing of a *yāḷa* of seed (paddy) in Kirivavula within the township of Siṅguruvāṇa, (an extent of) fields (sufficient for) the sowing of six *yāḷas* of seed (paddy) in New Badalagoḍa, which has been established by the construction anew of channels and a dam by us, our chiefs (mudali) and the host conjointly, (an extent of field sufficient for) the sowing of five *yāḷas* of seed (paddy) in Old Badalagoḍa and lands appertaining thereto, including trees and forests, (an extent of field sufficient for) the sowing of a *yāḷa* of seed (paddy) from Gonvāṇika in Sitdavulla, granted by Senā-Laṁkā-adhikāra from among the heritable lands belonging to him; (an extent of fields sufficient for) the sowing of a *yāḷa* of seed (paddy) from Yakālla in Old Badalagoḍa granted from the property of Vasa Laṁkā-vari adhikāra; (an extent of field sufficient for) the sowing of a *yāḷa* of seed (paddy) from (the property) of Satruvan-patirāja in Kasambiliyāgoḍa; (an extent of field sufficient for) the sowing of a *yāḷa* of seed (paddy) from Nāramgoḍa which is a donation from Divāṇa; (an extent of) field (sufficient) for the sowing of twelve *amuṇas* of seed paddy from the property of Jayasiṁha-patirāja in Deltoṭa, (which field) extends from the edge of the stream called Sīlpänkandura up to the boundary of Saputala, one *maḍel-viṭiyela* from Santāṇa; an extent of field sufficient for the sowing of a *yāḷa* of seed paddy from Goḍavela dedicated as it was prepared by having dams constructed and the stumps and roots removed, and granted conjointly by everybody high and low in the two townships of Siṇguruvāṇa; housesites, trees and forests appertaining to the aforesaid lands altogether amounting to seventeen *yāḷas* and twelve *amuṇas* in accordance with their boundaries as of old; articles for common use fo the Saṅgha *(garu-bhāṇḍa)* including (vessels of) gold, silver, bronze and copper, offered by Senā-Laṁkā-adhikāra from his own properties; two hundred slaves, male and female, from among the slaves that he had acquired at marriage and slaves purchased; and four hundred head of cattle comprising neat cattle and buffaloes likewise offered by Senā-Laṁkā-adhikāra; the dues called *pideni-paṇam* settled so that one *paṇama* be given every year from a house, in consideration of the fact that this shrine was established by the people of Laṁkā in their own name, and for the purpose of improving what has been done and causing what has not been done to be done, of maintaining without cessation the offerings of cooked rice, flowers and lamps to the Buddha and the gods, and for conducting audiences; a levy of a quarter per cent, at the Inner Customs House and the Outer Customs House, of the value of whatever merchandise purchased or sold by merchants coming from the nine seaports or the eighteen countries in accordance with the agreement engraved on copper and granted—all this has been settled (on this *vihāra*) with the stipulation that all revenues, including the goods received as above, shall be divided into five shares, out of which three shares shall appertain to the Three Jewels, (i.e. the Buddha, the Dhamma and the Saṇgha), one share to the gods and one share to any person descended in the succession of sons and grandsons of this Senā-Laṁkā-adhikāra, who is attached to this establishment and maintains it.

Should there be any persons who contravene anything from these as stated above, and forcibly appropriate anything through avarice, they will be born in the four evil states of existence such as hells, and will not be able to see Mete Budun (the future Buddha Maitreya); like crows and dogs they will not abtain food or drink, they will become more despised than the *caṇḍālas* and will become the sons of crows and dogs. Should there be any noble persons who, having known this, and in view of the scriptural text which says "Whosoever takes away anything out of the possession of the Buddha, be it a blade of grass, a stick of wood, a single flower or a fruit, he will become a monstrous goblin", wish to enjoy happiness both in this world and in the other world, who not desiring anything out of this, support this meritorious action even by a mere word or a mere letter, improve what has been done, cause to be done what has not been done and maintain (it)—should there be such high-souled persons—they will share in this meritorious action just as they themselves have done it, and realise the happiness of Heaven and the happiness of Nirvāṇa. And to that end and in order that this act of merit may be maintained in the future, this edict has been granted by me named Bhuvanaikabāhu, having had it recorded on copper-plates and in this stone inscription.

Therefore, Senā-Laṁkā-adhikāra, too, makes an exhortation of this manner. 'Whoever be the protector of this charitable endowment, Lord Senā-Laṁkādhikārin places the dust on his (i.e. that person's) two feet like a flower on his owen head.' 'Should this act of merit be protected, having rendered support to it even with a mere word or a letter by any noble person, the dust on the illustrious feet of that eminent personage is honoured by me, named Senā-Laṁkā-adhikāra, by having it placed on my head as if it were a cluster of fragrant flowers'.

'(This minister) of diverse splendour, in order to protect this charity of many forms, having contracted his fingers on his head, beseeches (to that end) lords of men, powerful ministers and other personages who are already born or will be born in the future.'

'So that this complete charity may be protected by noble kings who are already born, noble kings who will be born, noble ministers who are already born and noble ministers who will be born, and that this charity may be protected by the members of the hosts possessing splendour and prosperity, by me, named Senā-Laṁkā-adhikāra, they are beseeched having saluted them, placing on my head my two hands with their ten nails brought together'.

May there be happiness for the whole world."

2. Report of the Temple Land Commissioners 1857–1858, "Temple and Dewale Tenures"

The following text is taken from the first report of the temple land commission which is the most important source on the organization of Buddhist temples in Central Ceylon during the first half of the 19th century.

"Having thus briefly noticed the Rules which we deemed it necessary to lay down for our guidance, and the grounds on which we have been led to adopt them, we take this opportunity of submitting for the information of Government, a few particulars with reference to the tenures of Temple Lands, and the degree in which the relations between the Temples and their tenants have been affected by the great social and Governmental changes, which have taken place since the British accession.

At first sight, this might appear out of place in a Report of this kind, but we think it but right that the Government should be placed in possession of the true state of the case, and the results of the experience gained in the course of an enquiry extending over two years, and in different parts of the Kandian Provinces; and we feel that the following statement regarding the tenures of the lands of Temples and Dewales will prove interesting, if not conducive to practical benefit.

Dedicated lands are divided into *Muttettus* and *Nilepanguas*, or service shares, that is, lands held for the performance of certain services by their holders, who are called Nillecareas.

The Muttettus are of two classes. The first, where the whole, or a large portion of the lands of a village were dedicated by the King, or, with his permission, by the Chief to whom they belonged. In this case, the fields which were the absolute property of the dedicator, became the Muttettu of the Temple, or Dewale, and in general the tenants who held the other fields were bound to cultivate these without hire, the work being divided amongst them, some furnishing buffaloes for ploughing, some fencing the fields, and so on through all the necessary operations, until the whole crop, without deduction was placed free of expense in the Temple or Dewale granary.

The other class of Muttettus is where only a few amunams of paddy land, the immediate property of the donor, were dedicated, without any service shares being attached to them. These are given in ande to tenants, who either cultivate the whole land in one lot, and give a share, generally one-half, to the Temple, or cultivate a fixed portion of the field and take the crop of it, working the remainder for the Wihare and giving the produce to it. If the Muttettus had any high lands belonging to them, the chenas were cultivated by the tenants, who gave the ottu share, generally one-tenth, to the proprietor of the Muttettu. This class of Muttettus was principally dedicated to the local Wihares, which could profit by the produce, but seldom to the Dewales, for reasons which will be mentioned hereafter.

The service lands are also divided into two classes, *Parewaney*, or hereditary, and *Maruwene*, or transferable.

The dedication of Parewaney lands by the Kind, or by any other person with his permission, was not an absolute bestowal of the lands, but rather a resignation in favor of the Temple of the services which their hereditary possessors as land holders, owed to the King as Lord of the soil. As has been already mentioned, those tenants whose service it was to take a certain part in the cultivation of the fields which were the absolute property of the donor, continued to render the same service under the Temple; and all other services, generally, were transferred in the same manner. It is admitted that under the Kandian rule, the ejectment of Parewany tenants was not permitted without reference to the King, who never entirely resigned his rights as Lord Paramount, and it was never done unless a clear refusal to perform service was distinctly proved. It is stated that, in some cases, when the priest was powerful enough to secure the assistance or connivance of the Dissawe of the Province, it was done; and instances have occurred in which, when the priest had ejected a Parewany tenant, the Dissawe reinstated him by force; but that these cares were rare.

The second class of *Maruwene Nilepanguas*, are service lands which have been dedicated for some specific purpose, such as supplying a certain quantity of oil to light the Temple during festivals, etc. and are held by tenants-at-will. A portion of these are still held on the original tenure, but in consequence of the great changes which have taken place in the supply market, since the Kandian time, a great proportion of the lands of this class, belonging to the large Temples and Dewales, are now let in ande, or for a money rent, and the articles, for the supply of which they were dedicated, are purchased in the bazaars. Some of the Maruwene panguas in Udunuere are let to Moor bazaarkeepers in Kandy who supply a certain number of candles or gallons of oil yearly to the establishment from which they hold them.

These tenures are common to all religious property, but the relative proportion in which the different classes of dedications were made to Temples, is very different from that which they exhibit in the case of Dewales;and the reason of this is obvious, when the different constitution of their establishments is considered.

Those of Temples were local, and their members bound by a vow of poverty. Consequently, Muttettus of both classes were given to them to an extent sufficient to support the resident priests, and were in proportion to their number. Their *Pareweny Nillecareas* were just sufficient in number to cultivate the Muttettus, store the crop, and keep the buildings in repair, and their *Maruwene Nilepanguas*, large enough to furnish oil for lighting the Temple, or any other necessaries which the Muttettus could not supply, and to provide for the services of tom-tom beaters, horn-blowers, etc. Latterly, many of these services have been performed by Parewany Nillecareas.

The Dewale establishments, on the contrary, were not merely small local ones, but under the Kandian Kings they formed, collectively, a kind of "imperium in imperio," maintained for a political purpose. The dedications to them were therefore made not merely to an extent sufficient to supply the articles and attendance necessary for the performance of the ceremonies at the local Dewale, but for the maintenance of a number of lay chiefs, who ranked next to the Royal Dissawes, and required a corresponding retinue. Their revenue establishment had its staff of *Mohattales*, *Lecams*, etc., just as the Government Revenue Department had, and their personal retinues were of course large, at a time when the importance of an official was estimated by the number of his "following." Besides the personal attendants, and messengers of the Dewale Chiefs, it was necessary to provide guards for the local attuas, and for those at the principal station, and carriers to transport grain from the former to the latter; and to supply all these, large tracts of land were dedicated, with the tenants of which the Royal Officers never interfered, expect in cases of public emergency.

We have not been able to ascertain, whether their executive powers were formally recognized; but whether authorised or not, they were to a certain extent exercised, and in remote Districts, cases have occurred lately, in which tenants have been punished by fine and imprisonment, for non-performance of services, and even for disobedience of orders, by the Dewale officers. It is now generally admitted, that the large Dewale establishments were encouraged and supported by the Kandian Kings, rather from financial and political reasons, than from religious feeling; financial because each *Basnaike-Nilleme*, paid a large sum on appointment, and a further monthly payment while he remained in office, (as before stated, we have not been able to ascertain if this rule was general, and the evidence we have taken on the subject, goes to shew that the Basnaike-Nillemeweru of the Haterewarandeyo in Kandy, did not pay it; but it is admitted that the privincial Basnaike-Nillemeweru did); and political, as forming a useful check on the ambition of the Dissawes, as no general disaffection could have existed in their provinces, without the knowledge of the Dewale authorities. Keeping these facts in view, we can explain, why the position of Temple tenants is different from that of those holding under the Dewales, and how the gradual change which has taken place within the last forty years, from a state of semi-barbarous despotism to one of comparative civilization and freedom, has affected each.

In the case of Temples, there is in almost every village in which land is registered as Temple property, whether belonging to the Malwatte or Asgeria colleges, or to a local establishment, a village Wihare and Pansele, and one or more resident priests, by whom the village Temple lands are managed. Their tenants do not now pay to these priests the same blind and unhesitating obedience which they did under the Kandian rule, when a simple representation made by the priest to the *Dissawe* or *Maha Nilleme*, was sufficient to entail punishment, against which there was no appeal except to the King, by whom the sufferer was probably referred to the Dissawe, who had been a party to its infliction. It is now generally believed in the country, that it had been ruled in a late decision of the Supreme Court, that Parewany tenants could not be ejected, even for non-performance of services, and that the Temple had no resource except a Civil action to recover the value of the services withheld. We do not know if such a decision has been recorded, but we mention the general belief in it, as shewing what the people conceive their legal liabilities as tenants to be, and it is evident that the existence of such a belief must have a considerable effect on the priest's conduct as landlord, and make it his interest to be mild and indulgent to his tenants, inasmuch as it renders him dependent on their good feeling for the performance of all those services, to which they may not feel themselves legally bound. To shew this more clearly, we shall take the case of each class of lands separately. In the case of the first class of Muttettus, the priest, if he be popular, has his fields well cultivated, the produce carefully stored, and his Pansele comfortably thatched and repaired into the bargain. If he is unpopular, the Nillecarea who holds his lands by giving buffaloes for ploughing, does not find it convenient to give them on the day on which the man whose service it is to plough is ready to commence work, or vice versa, and against this and many other similar ways of annoying and injuring, of which we only give this as an example, the priest knows that he has no redress except by a suit at law, in which he will probably find it difficult to prove his exact loss, or, if there is a combination among the tenants, to throw the onus on any particular person.

Of the second class of Muttettus, which have no service lands for their cultivation attached to them, the priest, if influencial, can generally secure the whole crop also, the villagers voluntarily assembling and cultivating them as a work of merit, and depositing all the grain in the Wihare granary, without any hire except their food, on the days on which they are actually employed. If the priest has not sufficient influence to persuade them to do this, he must let these fields in ande, the cultivator giving a share, generally one half, to the Wihare, and keeping the other. In fact, if the priest be popular, he obtains the whole produce of his Muttettus of both classes. The cultivators of the Maruwene Nilepanguas pay with good measure the supplies due for their lands, and all join cheerfully in making up the deficiency there may be, and in keeping the building in order. If he is unpopular, he has to let out, possibly all his Muttettus certainly those of the second class, in ande, whereby he reduces his income by one half at once, the andecareas will simply give their ande share, if they will even do that fairly, and the priest has to hire labour himself for the repairs of his Wihare and Pansele.

Besides this, the esteem in which a priest is held by the tenants, is generally the measure of his popularity with the rest of the villagers, and upon this the amount of offerings at the festivals, wich is an important item in the revenue of a Temple, entirely depends. There are, of course, cases in which the supposed sanctity of the place, and not the character of the incumbent, is the motive, but these are exceptions, and do not affect the argument derived from the other cases, which form the rule.

Besides the relation in which the priests stand to their tenants, as landlords, and the religious influence of their profession, they have other holds on the affection of the people. Their Pansales are the schools for the village children, and the sons of even the superior Headmen are very generally educated at them. They have also, frequently, some knowledge of Medicine, and when this is the case, they generally give the benefit of their advice gratuitously, which the Vederales seldom do. Add to this that, as every revenue officer who has ever attempted to induce the natives to exert themselves for their own good knows, the priests are, generally, when properly applied to, foremost with their money, if rich, or with their influence or both, in furthering every scheme for local improvement, and from what has been stated, it will be evident, that not only is it their interest to be kind and considerate to their tenants, but that they generally are so, and that their influence among the people is, in a social point of view, usefully employed.

That the case is very different with the Dewales, will be evident from the following facts. There are four principal Dewales in the Kandian Provinces. The Maha, Nate, and Pattiny in Kandy, and the Kateregam Dewale, the principal station of which is at Kateregam, at these stations most of the principal Officers of the Dewales generally reside. The Basnaikenillemeweru, Mohattals and some of the Vidhanes live at the station, and seldom leave it to visit their villages, except those in their immediate neighbourhood, a few of the subsidiary Dewales, also, where the station is large enough to ensure a considerable amount of offerings, or the lands are extensive and profitable enough to make them worth looking after closely, have a staff of officers attached to them. Of the former class are the Kateregam Dewales of Badulla and Kandy, and of the latter the Kateregam Dewale of Embecca, the Nate Dewale of Wegiria, and some others. With such exceptions as these, all the village Dewales are left in charge of a Capuralle, or hereditary priest of the "deyo," who is generally the largest tenant, and holds his lands as officiating priest. The village Dewale is generally a shed of a few feet square, which is kept up, solely because, under the Kandian rule, the lands of an abandoned Temple or Dewale reverted to the Crown, and it is, in four cases out of five, in a half ruinous state. The Basnaikenilleme, the head landlord, lives near Kandy or wherever the provincial Dewale may be, and the other officers purchase their appointments from him and reimburse themselves from the "nilecareas," when they can, and out of the offerings. In fact, there is just the same difference between Budhist priests and Dewale officers, that there is between resident and absentee landlords, and the results to the tenants are similar. We cannot better illustrate this than by describing the effects of their system of management, if it can be so called, on each class of lands which they hold, as we have already done in the case of the Temples.

With respect to the first class of Muttettus, there may be a few instances where they lie within a very short distance of the principal Dewale, in which the whole produce is given to the granary; but we have not in the course of our investigations met with a single case, in which this was done, where the fields lay more than a few miles from the station. The reason of this is obvious. There are not in the villages any officers who have a direct interest in attending to their cultivation, while, in some cases, the interest of the villagers may, and in others must be, antagonistic to those of the Dewale. For instance, a man is not likely to sacrifice a favorable season for cultivating his own field for the sake of attending first to the interests of the Dewale, or to give his buffaloes to plough the Muttettus, when he requires their services himself. These are some of the possible cases, but there are others which are certain. The tenants know, that if they cultivated the Muttettu to the best advantage, and got a large crop one year, they entailed on themselves the same care every year, at the risk, if they did not employ it, of exposing themselves to the charge, either of neglect of duty, or of pilfering. Again, the most burthensome duty which the tenants have to perform, is pounding the paddy in the Dewale granary, and carrying it to the principal station; and the larger the crop, the more heavily did this service fall upon them. From the circumstances which have been mentioned, and other similar ones, the natural result has followed, and the Dewales have found it more to their advantage to agree to terms which would make it the interest of the tenants to cultivate the Muttettu properly. In some cases, the fields are let out in ande, the Dewale share being a stated proportion of the crop. In others, and this is the plan now most generally adopted, the Dewale receives a fixed quantity of grain, whatever the crop may be, every time the field is cultivated; and, latterly, in some cases, the fields have been let for a money rent. We have met with some cases in which the rent is given partly in money and partly in kind.

The result of this change of system is, that those tenants who had to cultivate the Muttettus are entirely freed from that which was their most severe service, while those who were obliged to watch at the village attua, are no longer required to take their turn as guards. Thus the two heaviest, indeed the only heavy, local services, are at once taken off.

As has been before mentioned, the second class of Muttettus are comparatively seldom found in dedications to Dewales, so seldom, that it is unnecessary to take them into consideration here, and the Maruwene Nilepanguas are in general let for a small rent either in money or in kind.

In the case of the Pareweny tenants, those who cultivated the Dewale Muttettus and guarded the atuas, have been entirely relieved from these services. Those whose duty it was to attend as messengers, guards, etc., at the principal atua, and on the Dewale chiefs, have for years ceased to do so; and this latter class is said to comprise about four-fifths of the whole number of tenants. And in fact, of the fixed services which were exacted under the Kandian rule, almost the only ones which are now performed are, conveying the Dewale share of grain from the village atuas to the principal station, furnishing guards, tom-tom beaters, etc., to the Dewale there, attending at the festivals, (on which occasions they take a present to the Dewale chiefs, and officers) and, at rare intervals, assisting in the repairs of some of the buildings.

It might naturally be inferred, that duties so slight, when divided amongst a tenantry of several thousands, would fall lightly upon each individual, as, in fact, they would, if divided equally amongst them; but to do this would involve more trouble, and a better system of management than the Dewale officers employ, and they find it easier to exact ten times the amount of service from those tenants who reside at short distances from them, than to compel those who live 20, 30 or 50 miles from the Dewale, to bear their just share of the burden. The consequence is, that in all the villages within ten or fifteen miles of the principal station you meet with a tenantry who complain loudly of the exaction of services which are not due, and of extortion and neglect of interests, and who are therefore eager to be released from the authority of the Dewale, and to be allowed to pay tax to Government; while in the more remote villages, the tenants, though obliged to admit that they perform merely nominal services, if any, leave no means untried to prove their right to be considered Dewale tenants, and so to escape taxation. Thus a number of the Nilecareas are harassed and oppressed, while we have large communities scattered through the country possessing whole villages, and sometimes even whole Aratchiewasams, in the anomalous position of rendering no services to the Dewales for their land, paying no tax to Government, assuming an independence of the headmen, and carrying that assumption, on all possible occasions, as far as they safely can, unless he happens also to hold an appointment under the Dewale; an anomalous state of things, and well calculated, in a semi-civilized community, to create a fretting and discontented feeling among the remainder of the population, who are far differently circumstanced.

Nor does the evil, as regards the few villages from which all the real services are exacted, stop here. At the time of the establishment of village Dewales, each was an independent establishment, and its tenants performed their services at the local Dewale of their own village. This was so much easier than the Government Rajekaria, by which the people were often taken to a distance from their homes, and obliged to remain absent for a considerable time, that it became a common practice for the land owners of a village to build a small Dewale and dedicate their lands to it; by doing which they freed themselves from services to the Crown. This was at last carried to such an extent, as to begin to affect the number of people required for Government services; and the King, to check it, without by so doing incurring the charge of irreligion, ordered all the tenants of village Dewales to perform their services at the principal Dewale of the "deyo," to whom their village one was dedicated. By this change, instead of having to render a nominal daily attendance at their village Dewale for a month or so every year, in their turn, they found themselves obliged to reside for that period in Kandy, or wherever the principal station might be; and it is stated that this, as it naturally would do, put a stop to village dedications.

Another account which is given of the change is, that the Basnaikenillemes of the principal Dewales, represented to the King that they had not a sufficient number of tenants in their neighbourhood to enable them to perform the ceremonies with sufficient magnificence, and petitioned that the village tenants of the deyos might be ordered to attend also, but the former one seems to be most probable. Possibly both may be in part true, as the Basnaikenillemeweru, living at the Court, and dependent for their office on a despotic monarch, would, probably, have acted on his slightest hint.

The result of this is, that a certain number of tenants from each of the villages in which there is a subsidiary Dewale near the principal station, are obliged to reside for a certain time, varying from one to six months, every year, at that station, and while there, leading as they do, a perfectly idle life, they very frequently fall into habits of gambling and inebriety, which they carry back with them to their villages.

The effects of this may easily be calculated, and the result of our own observations is, that the people of the Dewale villages, the tenants of which are obliged to perform their services in Kandy, are the most corrupt and disorderly in the Kandian Provinces. Another way in which the periodical residence of the villagers in Kandy tends to the same injurious result is, that they often, in the beginning of their gambling career, lose money to low country men of the worst class, to whom, in payment, they sell their village lands; and in one village in the Gangepalate of Udunuere, a case came to light, during the investigation of the Dewale claims, in which the Dewale henea had, while performing service in Kandy, sold, piece by piece, all his Paraweny land (and he had originally been comparatively rich) except a small paddy field, which he led in ande to some other villagers, while he lived entirely in Kandy, supporting himself by his trade and by gambling. This is far from being a solitary instance, and in all the Dewale villages in the neighbourhood of Kandy, the more respectable of the older inhabitants speak with disgust of the vicious habits, which the young men acquire during their turn of service in Kandy.

There is but little doubt that the exaction of services other than those on which the lands were originally held, will sooner or later produce its own remedy, as it appears questionable, whether the landlord having waived the regular service without at the time stipulating for the performance of others in their stead, can now enforce the performance of any except those customarily due, and from what we have seen of the feeling of the tenants, we are disposed to think, that if one tenant were to resist successfully, his example would be followed by all others in a very short time. Should this happen, the inhabitants of the villages in the neighbourhood of Kandy would have as little to do as their more fortunate confreres of the distant districts.

That we have not exaggerated the freedom from service of many of the Dewale villages, the following extract from the evidence of the Capurale of the Hangurankette Pattiny Dewale, will shew.

"Attenaikemudianselagey Punchierale Capurale, affirmed, states—

"The Nillecareas used to cultivate the Muttettu fields; that was their principal service. They have not done so for about fifteen years. Since the appointment of the present Basnaikenilleme I do not know how much land we have altogether. The Nillecareas scarcely perform any service now, except repairing the Dewale, and attending at the festivals. Some of them do not even come to the festivals. Some of them do not do a day's work in each year. The Basnaikenilleme comes twice a year, and the Panaidecareas (11 of them) have to furnish each five measures of rice per day, and six ridies. These men do no other services to the Dewale. The Dewale is falling. The Nillecareas are not made to perform services, and the Muttettu fields are let on rent to strangers, who pay the rent to the Basnaikenilleme, and he never disburses a pice for the upkeep of the Temple. There is some money also collected at the Pereheras, and all this the Basnaikenileme takes away for better security. I know that, from as long as I recollect up to seventeen years ago, the Nillecareas performed services and cultivated the Muttettu fields."

"The six Paindecareas of Allewattugame do no service, except to the Basnaikenileme. I never saw them at the Dewale. There are eight Nillecareas. They do no work except carry flags at the Perehera. There are eight watchers. They have each thirty days in each year. Besides this, there is one man who furnishes honey to the Walawe."

"In Walewele there are no Nillecareas or Paindecareas. There is a Gammahei and a Henea. That was all there used to be, but the present Basnaikenilleme has appointed a Berecarea. The Gammahei thatches a part of the Dewale and gives foor amunams and two pelas of paddy per year, and attends fifteen days at the Perehera. The Henea ties clothes at the four festivals, and has to give me a clean cloth every eighth day. The Berecarea has to beat tom-toms at the four festivals, and thatch his share of the Dewale. None of these three help to cultivate the Muttettu fields which are given in ande."

This is the only case in which it has been proved, that the tenants were directly ordered not to perform services, but, as an almost universal rule, in the distant villages, they have gradually been allowed to neglect them, and their case may be briefly described. Some entire villages, whose tax, if fairly commuted, would amount to from 10l. to 15l. per annum, each send a few shillings a year, or their equivalent in oil, etc. Of some, the tenants go to Kandy, once a year, for one of the festivals, and take a present of rice or betel to the Basnaikenilleme, and the very great majority perform no services at all, and this is not to be wondered at, when we know that, even under the Kandian rule, the distant nillecareas required to be driven in by the Dissawe, and that, after the accession, it appears from the Diaries of the Board of Commissioners for the Kandian Provinces, that Native officers of Government were sometimes ordered to send in the tenants of Dewale villages to perform their Rajekaria in Kandy.

To sum up the result of our observations on this point in a few words:

1. There may be some Dewale Nillecareas who perform regularly all the services for which they hold their lands, but, in the course of our enquiries, extending over a large part of the Central Province, we have not found one who did.

2. About one-tenth of the whole number of tenants, although not performing the services for which they are legally liable, perform others which are equivalent, or more than equivalent, in value.

3. Of the remaining nine-tenths, about one-fifth of the whole perform services which are of some, although very trifling, actual value. One-fifth more attend at some of the festivals, a service which is of no real value, and only adds to the eclat of the ceremonies; and the remainder perform no services at all.

It follows, from what has been stated, that the services nominally due by the Tenants of Dewales are very irregularly performed, and that, in a social point of view, the result of this is very injurious to the tenants themselves,—some of whom are ground down by services, oppressive in their action, and demoralizing in their effects, while others enjoy a perfect immunity from every kind of impost, and are thus encouraged in a life of utter idleness.

The Rajekaria, or compulsory service due to the King, abolished in 1832, was also, though in a less degree, unequal in its operation. Its commutation for a fixed payment, penalized the burthen incumbent on all, and unquestionably improved the condition of the people, who would dread, now, the restoration of a power which was so frequently convertible into an instrument of oppression. A similar commutation of Temple and Dewale services, is, we think, a subject well worthy the consideration of Government, and might with propriety be made the subject of negociation with the Temple and Dewale authorities.

There can be little doubt, that they could readily be brought to see, that the interests of their Temples would be better served by a fixed payment, recoverable by a simple process at law, than by an uncertain service, nominally compulsory, but actually difficult even of definition, and often incapable of enforcement; while the social condition of their tenants, a large section of the Kandian community, would be thus raised and ameliorated."

GLOSSARY

ādāhanaya maluva	cremation ground, royal cremation ground in Kandy
adukkuva	dressed provisions, "rice and curry"
ālatti	offering of lights to the Buddha, a deity or a King
ālattiammā	woman performing ālatti service in a temple
alukesel	ash-plantain (fruit)
alut sahal mangalaya	the "new rice festival" in January each year, one of the four principle temple festivals
amuṇa	measure of land in sowing extent. 1 amuṇa equals 4 päl
ānamēsera	decorations used at temple festivals
anda	share of crop (usually one half)
äpā	crown-prince
ārakkhaka	guardian of a sanctuary, appointed by the King (Anurādhapura period)
ārāmaya	Buddhist monastery
aramudalgē	treasury house
Asgiri Vihāraya	the Asgiriya Monastery in Kandy, center of the Asgiriya Chapter *(pārśvaya)* of the Siyam Nikāya
ätul kaṭṭalē	inner chamber of a temple (regarded as ritually clean)
ätulkaṭṭalē rājakārikaranāya	persons performing temple service in the inner chambers
aṭapirikara	eight articles required by a Buddhist monk
avurudu mangalaya	New Year festical
badda	department of the Kandyan administration, organized on a caste basis
baḍahälayā	potter, man of potter's caste
badu mila	rents
bamuṇu kula	Brahmin caste
banagē	preaching hall of a Buddhist temple
banamaduva	see banagē
baṇḍāra	son of chief, prince
bāraya	1. vow made to a god; 2 care, charge, custody
basnāyaka nilamē	temple lord in charge of a dēvālaya
beravāyā	drummer, man of drummer's caste
beraya	drum, "tom-tom"
dāgaba	Dagoba, monument usually containing a relic of the Buddha or one of his disciples
Daḷadā Māḷigāva	Temple of the Tooth in Kandy
dāna	offering of a meal to Buddhist monks
dānṣālāva (dangē)	dining room in a Buddhist monastrye
dāyaka sabhāva	society of lay donors to a temple
dēvālaya	Temple of a God or Gods
dēvālagama	temple land, belonging to a dēvālaya; temple village; temple estate
deviyā (dēvayā)	God

diggē	the long hall, hall of drummers in a temple
diyagē	water closet
diyavaḍana nilamē	Chief administrator, trustee, temple lord of the Temple of the Tooth in Kandy
durāva	1. Toddy-tapper caste; 2. Kandyan service caste
durayā	1. Chief of a low caste; 2. chief of the paduva caste; 3. Kandyan service caste
durutu māsaya	the month of January-February
gabaḍāgama	royal village, royal estate
gabaḍāgē (gabaḍāva)	granary, royal or temple storehouse
gamarāla	village headman
gamavasama	land held by village headman or by temple officials
gebanarāla	storekeeper, officer of the treasure house
gebarāla	temple store-keeper
gepalanarāla	"temple master," keeper of temple keys
gilanpasa	light refreshment taken by Buddhist monks in the afternoon or evening
gilan pasa pūjāva	evening offering in a vihāraya
gōvāgeḍiya	cabbage
goyigama	farmer, man of the farmer's caste
hakgediya	conch shell, blown to signal the beginning and end of temple rituals
handun	sandal wood
hēlaya	piece of cloth
hēnayā	washerman, dhobi; man of washermen's caste
hēvisiya	"drum roar," temple music
hīldānaya	morning offering at a vihāraya
hī lēkam miṭiya	Register of ploughed lands in the Kandyan Kingdom
hūniyama	magic, sorcery, enchantment by spells
kācci mangalaya	see Kārtika mangalaya
kapurāla	priest of the Gods, serving at a dēvālaya
karavala	dried salt-fish
kārtika mangalaya	temple festival of lights, celebrated on the fullmoon day of the month of Kārtika (November-December)
kataragama	one of the major deities, venerated by the Sinhalese
kat hāl rājakāriya	grain-tax during Kandyan period, reckoned in pingo loads
kātti mangalaya	see Kārtika mangalaya
kävili	cakes, pastry, sweetmeats
kenmura	days of Gods (Wednesday and Saturday in Kandy District), days on which offerings to gods are made
koḍiya	flag, banner
kumārayā	prince
kūruva	Department of Elephants in the Kingdom of Kandy
lāha	measure of land according to sowing extent = kuruṇiya
Lankātilaka	Lankātilaka Temple in Udunuvara, Kandy District

laukika	pertaining to this world, mundane, worldly
liṅga	phallic symbol of Siva
lōkōttara	1. pertaing to the next world, otherworldly; 2. king, sovereign
magul	auspicious occasion, good fortune, festival; marriage, marriage ceremony; royal
maha gamvasama	"great official land"; land held by certain temple officials
mahānāyaka	head of a chapter of monks (nikāya or pārśvaya)
Mahanuvara	Kandy (lit. "great city")
māḷigāva	palace, Temple of the Tooth in Kandy (Daladā Māligāva)
malvatta vihāraya	"Flower Garden Monastery" in Kandy, center of the Malvatta Chapter (parsvaya) of the Siyam Nikāya
mānagamvasama	"Measurer's official land," held by a temple official
maṅgalaya	festival, temple festival, marriage feast
māruvena panguva	non-hereditary share of temple land, temple land which may be allocated to tenants at the temple lord's will
mīgondena panguva	"buffalo share" (of temple land)
multän	food prepared for the Buddha or the Gods
multänrāla also: mulutänrāla	cook of offerings
mulutän	*see* multän
mura	shift (of temple service)
mutteṭṭuva	land owned by a temple and worked by temple tenants
mutukuḍē or: mutukuḍaya	pearl umbrella, emblem of royalty or devine status
näkata	auspicious time, polite term for man of drummer's caste, astrologer's sub-caste
nānumura	ritual of purification by cleaning the reflection of the Buddha image or the image of a God in a mirror
Nātha	one of the principal gods, venerated by the Sinhalese, lit. lord
nilakārayā	tenant of temple land, temple servant
nilavasama	land held by temple tenants
nindagam	"lands of a lord", usually of the Kandyan aristocracy (radala)
paduvā	caste of "palanquin-bearers"
päla	a measure of land according to sowing extent
paliha	shield
pandama	torch
panḍuru mila	money offering to a temple
panguva	share, share of temple land
pangukārayā	holder of a paraveni panguva (heritary share of vihāragama or dēvālagama)
panikkalayā	drummer, tom-tom beater
panikkayā	chief of a low caste, elephant keeper, barber
pansala	dwelling of monks, monastery

paramparāva	lineage, line of succession, esp. from teacher to pupil in the Buddhist monkhood, "ordination lineage".
paravēni	ancestral (implying permanent title to land)
pārśvaya	"chapter" of a nikāya of the Buddhist monkhood
paṭabändā	holder of gamvasama, holder of a honorific title given by a Sinhalese King
paṭabändinama	honorific title
pātimokkha	rules of conduct for Buddhist monks, contained in the Vinaya Piṭaka
Pattini	goddess venerated by the Sinhalese
payinḍakārayā	messanger, person appointed to transmit orders of the temple lord or temple headman to temple tenants
payinḍakiyana gamvasama	"messenger's official land", temple land held by temple messenger for his services
pēhimiya	lord of demons
penuma	"appearance," present given by temple tenants to the temple lord
perahära	procession, temple festival
perahära vīdiya	procession street
pilimagē	image house, temple
pin	religious merit
piṭakaṭṭalē	"outer services" at a devalaya
piṭisara	"outer temples," temples connected with the four major Kandy temples
pirita	verses chanted by Buddhist monks for protection from evil spirits, demons and misfortune
piruvaṭa	ritually clean cloth provided by washerman (e.g. so temple officials)
pohoya	quarter days of the moon, weekly Buddhist holidays
pōyagē	building in a Buddhist monastery, sanctified by a formally established boundary (sīma) and used for higher ordination ceremonies (uposampadā) and recitations of the pātimokkha
Prātimōkṣaya	*see* Pātimokkha
prāsāda	temple, residence of a king
pravēṇi *see:* paravēṇi	
puhulgeḍiya	ash pumpkin, used for offerings to demons
pūjāva	offering to a God (dēva pūjāva) or to the Buddha (Buddha pūjāva)
puññakkhetta	merit-field
radala	Kandyan aristocracy, subcaste of goyigama caste
radavā	washerman, man of washerman's caste
raja	king
rājakāriya	service due to the king, a lord or a temple; "temple service" done by temple tenants
ranāyudha	weapon or insignia of a god

randōli	palanguin, in which the insignia or weapons of a god are carried during temple festivals
raṭa	district, country
sāmaṇera	novice in the Buddhist monkhood
sangha	Buddhist monkhood, order, group of Buddhist monks
sanghārāmaya	Buddhist monastery
Senālaṅkādhikāra	chief minister of King Bhuvanaikabahu IV of Gampola and founder of Lankātilaka Temple
sīmāva	boundary, formally established by the Sangha. Within the boundary important rituals can be validly performed
siṅhāsanaya	thronehouse at end of the procession street of a temple
sisildānaya	morning offering at a vihāraya; morning meal of a Buddhist monk
Śiṣyānu śiṣya paramparāva	pupilary succession from monkteacher to pupil, rule of succession to the office of chief monk (vihārādhipati) of a Buddhist monastery
Śrīpādasthānaya	Adam's Peak with the Buddha's footprint, important pilgrim place
Syāma Nikāya syāmopālivaṁsika)	the "Siamese Order" of Buddhist monks in Ceylon. The order traces its ordination tradition to Thailand
tala atta	branch of talipot palm
talapata	palm-leaf umbrella
tammätan	kettle drum
taṭṭumāru	system of rotating cultivation of a jointly owned parcel of paddy land
tēvāva	ritual of washing and fanning
timbili	Kandyan subcaste of the goyigama caste
torana	arch constructed for festivals and processions
tuḍapata	land-grant recorded on an ola leaf
udavikārayā	helper, assistant
upasampadāva	higher ordination of a Buddhist monk
väḍavasam	service tenure
vahalkaḍa	entrance hall to a temple
valankada	pingo-pot
valavva	house of a member of the Kandyan aristocracy (radala), manor
vaṇṇakurāla	temple accountant
vatarāla	attendant at temple rituals
vattakāraka	guardian, caretaker, attendant
vatterurāla *see* vatarāla	
vaṭṭōruva	list

Vibhīṣaṇa	God venerated by the Sinhalese
vidāna	temple official, (in Kandyan times village official)
vihārādhipati	chief monk of a Buddhist monastery, often a "monastic landlord"
vihāragam	temple land of a Buddhist temple (vihāraya) which is either owned by the temple or for which services (rājakāriya) are due to the temple
vihāraya	Buddhist temple
Viṣṇu	one of the principal gods venerated by the Sinhalese
viyāraṇ	assurance
yāla	1. measure of land in sowing extent, 1 yāla = 12 amunu; 2. second harvest season for paddy
yakā	demon

BIBLIOGRAPHY

Abbreviations

AA	American Anthropologist
BEFEO	Bulletin de l'Ecole Français d'Extrême-Orient
CALR	Ceylon Antiquary and Literary Register
CJHSS	Ceylon Journal of Historical and Social Studies
EZ	Epigraphia Zeylanica
JAS	Journal of Asian Studies
JCBRAS	Journal of the Ceylon Branch of the Royal Asiatic Society
JRAI	Journal of the Royal Anthropological Institute
SP	Sessional Papers (Government of Ceylon)
UCR	University of Ceylon Review

Aluwihare, Sir Richard
1964 The Kandy Perahera.
Colombo: M. D. Gunasena.

Ames, Michael M.
1962 "Popular Ideology and Village Rites of the Sinhalese Buddhists"
Paper read at the University of Wisconsin symposium on Buddhist Studies.
1963 "Ideological and Social Change in Ceylon. Human Organization 22:45–53.
1964a "Magical-animism and Buddhism: A Structural Analysis of the Sinhalese System". JAS XXIII, special issue, 21–52.
1964b "Buddha and the Dancing Goblins: a Theory of Magic and Religion". AA 66:75–82.
1964c "Religion, Politics, and Economic Development in Ceylon: An Interpretation of the Weber Thesis".
Proceedings of the 1964 Annual Meeting of the American Ethnological Society.
1966 "Ritual Prestations and the Structure of the Sinhalese Pantheon".
Yale University Southeast Asia Studies, Cultural Report Series No. 13:27–50.

Barnett, L. D.
1917 Alphabetical Guide to Sinhalese Folklore from Ballad Sources.
Bombay: The British India Press.

Bareau, André
1957 La vie et l'organisation des communautés Bouddhiques modernes de Ceylon.
Pondichéry: Institut Français d'Indologie.

Bhattacharya, Kamelaswar
1961 Les religions brahmaniques dans l'ancien Cambodge.
Paris: Ecole Française d'Extrême-Orient, Vol. XLIX.
1955 Some Aspects of Temple Administration in the Ancient Khmer Kingdom.
Calcutta Review 134,2:193–199

Bechert, Heinz
1957 "Zur Geschichte der buddhistischen Sekten in Indien und Ceylon".
La Nouvelle Clio, 7–9: 311–360
1963 "Sanskrit Bildung und Schulsystem in Birma und Ceylon".
Wiener Zeitschrift für die Kunde Süd-und Ostasiens 7:1–12.
1966 Buddhismus, Staat und Gesellschaft in den Ländern des Theravāda-Buddhismus. Bd. 1, Allgemeines und Ceylon.
Frankfurt: Alfred Metzner Verlag. Bd. XVII/I der Schriften des Instituts für Asienkunde in Hamburg.
1967 Buddhismus, Staat und Gesellschaft in den Ländern des Theravāda-Buddhismus. Bd. 2, Birma, Kambodscha, Laos, Thailand. Wiesbaden: Otto Harrassowitz. Bd. XVIII/2 der Schriften des Instituts für Asienkunde in Hamburg.

BECHERT, Heinz
1968 "Einige Fragen der Religionssoziologie und Struktur des südasiatischen Buddhismus", Internationales Jahrbuch fuer Religionssoziologie, Bd. 4 Köln: Westdeutscher Verlag, 251–295.
BELL, H. C. P.
1892 Report on the Kegalle District of the Province of Sabaragamuva.
Colombo: Government Printers; Archaeological Survey of Ceylon, Sessional Paper XIX.
BROHIER, R. L.
1934–1935 Ancient Irrigation Works in Ceylon. 3 vols.
Colombo: Ceylon Government Press.
BUDDHIST COMMISSION OF INQUIRY
1956 The Betrayal of Buddhism.
Balangoda: Dharmavijaya Press.
CHADWICK, W. O.
1968 "Monasticism"
Int. Enc. Soc. Sc. 10:415–19
COEDÈS, G.
1911 "L'apotheose au Cambodge".
Bulletin de La Commission Archeologique de l'Indochine: 38–49.
1951 "La Divinisation de la Royante dans l'ancien Royaume Khmer à l'époque d'Angkor."
Proceedings of the VIIth International Congress for the History of Religions 1950.
CODRINGTON, H. W.
1933 "The Gampola Period in Ceylon History".
JCBRAS 32, No. 86: 260–309.
1938 Ancient Land Tenure and Revenue in Ceylon.
Colombo: Ceylon Government Press.
1947 A Short History of Ceylon.
London: Macmillan.
COOMARASWAMY, Ananda K.
1956 Mediaeval Sinhalese Art.
New York: Pantheon Books.
COPLESTON, Reginald Stephen.
1892 Buddhism, Primitive and Present in Magadha and in Ceylon.
London: Longmans.
CLOUGH, B.
1892 Sinhalese—English Dictionary.
Colombo: Wesleyan Mission Press.
Dambadeni Katikāvata
1266 A.C. ms.
DAVY, John
1821 An Account of the Interior of Ceylon and of its Inhabitants.
London: Longman, Hurst, Rees, Orme and Brown.
DE CASPARIS, J. G.
1961 "New Evidence on the Cultural Relations between Java and Ceylon in Ancient Times".
Artibus Asiae, XXIV: 241–48.
DERANIYAGALA, P. E. P. ed.
1954 Sinhala Verse (kavi).
Collected by the late Hugh Nevill, F.Z.S. (1869–1886).
Colombo: Government Press. Ceylon National Museums Manuscript Series Vol. V, Part 1 & 2.

DICKSON, J. F.
1884 "Notes Illustrative of Buddhism as the Daily Religion of the Buddhists of Ceylon, and some account of their ceremonies before and after Death".
JCBRAS 8: 207–231.
DIEHL, Carl Gustav
1956 Instrument and Purpose: Studies in Rites and Rituals in South India.
Lund: C. W. K. Gleerup.
DOUGLAS, Mary
1966 Purity and Danger: An Analysis of Concepts of Pollution and Taboo.
New York: Frederick A. Praeger.
DUMONT, Louis
1957 Une sous-caste de l'Inde du Sud: organization sociale et religion des Pramalai-Kaller.
La Haye: Mouton & Co.
1962 "The Conception of Kingship in Ancient India". Contributions to Indian Sociology VI: 48–77.
DUTT, Sukumar
1962 Buddhist Monks and Monasteries of India. Their History and Their Contribution to Indian Culture.
Lond: George Allen & Unwin Ltd.
EVERS, Hans-Dieter
1962 "Das Erziehungswesen als Faktor in der sozialen und wirtschaftlichen Entwicklung Ceylons", in H. N. Weiler, H. D. Evers et al., Erziehungswesen im sozialen Wandel.
Freiburg: Verlag Rombach: 24–36.
1963 "Buddhististische Gesellschaftsordnung und buddhistischer Wohlfahrtsstaat".
Moderne Welt, Vol. 4: 265–277.
1964a Kulturwandel in Ceylon: Eine Untersuchung über die Enstehung einer Industrie Unternehmerschicht.
Baden-Baden: Lutzeyer (Nomos), Sozialwissenschaftliche Beitrage zur Entwicklungsforschung, Band 1.
1964b "Buddhism and British Colonial Policy in Ceylon, 1815–1875".
Asian Studies, Vol. 2,3: 223–233.
1964c "Die soziale Organisation der singhalesischen Religion".
Kölner Zeitschrift für Soziologie. 16, 2:314–326.
1965 "Magic and Religion in Sinhalese Society".
American Anthropologist, 67, 1: 97–99.
1966 "Some Comparative Notes on the Organization of the Sangha in Ceylon and Siam".
Social Science Review. 4: 96–99. (Special number).
1967 "Kinship and Property Rights in a Buddhist Monastery in Central Ceylon"
American Anthropologist. Vol. 69, 6: 703–710.
1968a "Buddha and the Seven Gods: The Dual Organization of a Temple in Central Ceylon".
Journal of Asian Studies, 27, 2:541–550.
1968b "The Buddhist Sangha in Ceylon and Thailand: A Comparative Study of Formal Organizations in Two Non-Industrial Societies".
Sociologus, 18, 1:20–35.
1969 Loosely Structured Social Systems: Thailand in Comparative Perspective; New Haven, Yale University Southeast Asia Studies.
1969 "Monastic Landlordism in Ceylon: A Traditional System in a Modern Setting".
Journal of Asian Studies 28, 4:685–692.
FERNANDO, P. E. E.
1960 "India Office Land Grant of King Kīrti Srī Rājasiṃha"
CJHSS 3, 1:72–81.

GEIGER, Wilhelm
1960 Culture of Ceylon in Mediaeval Times.
Wiesbaden: Otto Harrassowitz.
GODAKUMBURA, C. E.
1955 Sinhalese Literature.
Colombo.
GOLOUBEW, V.
1933 "La Temple de la dent à Kandy".
BEFEO, 32: 441–474.
GONDA, I.
1966 Ancient Indian Kingship from the Religious Point of View.
Leiden: E. J. Brill.
GOONERATNE, Dandris de Silva.
1865 "On Demonology and Witchcraft in Ceylon".
JCBRAS 4: 1–117.
GOUGH, E. Kathleen
1960 "Caste in a Tanjore Village".
In E. R. Leach, ed. Aspects of Caste in South India, Ceylon and North-West Pakistan. Cambridge Papers in Social Anthropology No. 2.
GUNASEKARA, B.
1887 "Three Sinhalese Inscriptions: Text, Transliteration, Translation and Notes".
JCBRAS X, 34: 83–105.
HARDY, Robert Spence.
1860 Eastern Monachism.
Edinburgh: Williams and Norgate.
HAYLEY, Frederic Austin
1923 A Treatise on the Laws and Customs of the Sinhalese.
Colombo: H. W. Cave & Co.
HEINE-GELDERN, R. von
1930 "Weltbild und Bauform in Südost-Asien".
Wiener Beitrage zur Kunst und Kulturgeschichte Asiens, IV.
1956 "Conceptions of State and Kingship in Southeast Asia".
Cornell University Southeast Asia Program, Data Paper No. 18
HOCART, A. M.
1923 "Buddha and Devadatta".
Indian Antiquary 52: 267–272.
1931 The Temple of the Tooth in Kandy.
London: Lusac.
HOCART, A. M.
1926 "The Kandyan Lankātilaka".
Memoirs of the Archaeological Survey of Ceylon, Vol. 2: 18–21.
1928 "Duplication of Office in the Indian State".
The Ceylon Journal of Science,
Section G, Vol. 1, part 4: 205–210.
INDRAPALA, K.
1967 Review of S. Paranavitana, Ceylon and Malaysia.
JCBRAS XI: 101–106.
JAYATILAKA, Sir D. B.
1934 Saranankara, the Last Sangha-Raja of Ceylon.
Colombo: Lankabhinava Vissruta Press.
Kathinānisansa
n.d. (about 1420 A.C.), Neville Mss. No. 36, British Museum Library, Oriental Manuscript Collection.
KNOX, Robert
1681 An Historical Relation of Ceylon.
Reprinted 1958, Colombo: Ceylon Historical Journal, Vol. 6 (1956–57).

LAWRIE, Sir Archibald Campbell.
1896 A Gazetteer of the Central Province of Ceylon. 2 vols. Colombo: Government Printer.
LEACH, E. R.
1961 Pul Eliya, a Village in Ceylon: a Study of Landtenure and Kinship. Cambridge: Cambridge University Press.
1962 "Pulleyar and the Lord Buddha". Psychoanalysis and the Psychoanalytic Review, 49: 81–102.
LECLERE, A.
1916 Cambodge, fêtes civiles et religieuses. Paris.
LE MESURIER, C. J. R.
1881 "A Short History of the Principal Religious Ceremonies observed by the Kandyans of Ceylon". JCBRAS 7, 23:32–48.
1893 Manual of Nuwara Eliya District, Ceylon. Colombo: Government Printer.
LÉVY-STRAUSS, Claude
1963 Structural Anthropology, New York and London: Basic Books.
LINGAT, Robert.
1937 "Vinaya et Droit laique. Etudes sur les conflits de la loi religieuse et de la loi laique dans l'Indochine hinayaniste". BEFEO 37: 415–477.
Mahāvaṃsa, translated by W. Geiger.
n.d. Colombo: Government Press, various editions. (abbreviated as Mv).
MASPERO, M. George
1919 "La prière du bain des statues divines chez les Chams". BEFEO, 19, V.
1928 Le Royaume de Champa. Paris et Bruxelles: Librairie Nationale d'Art et d'Histoire. (Leiden: E.-J. Brill, 1914)
MASSON, Joseph.
1942 La Religion populaire dans le Canon Bouddhique Pali. Louvain: Bibliothèque du Museon.
MILLÄWA, Dissāva of Wellassa.
1817 "Account of the Kandy Äsela Perahära". Colombo: Ceylon Government Gazette September 13th, 1817. Reprinted in PIERIS, Ralph 1956: 135–138.
MUDIYANSE, Nandasena
n.d. The Art and Architecture of the Gampola Period (1341–1415 A.D.) Colombo: M. D. Gunasena (1965)
MULLER, Edward
1883 Ancient Inscriptions in Ceylon. London: Trubner.
Nompota (Manuscript)
n.d. British Museum, Wickramasinghe Catalogus: 31, III Fol. 11–12b.
NICHOLAS, C. W. and PARANAVITANA, S.
1961 A Concise History of Ceylon from the Earliest Times to the Arrival of the Portuguese in 1505. Colombo: Ceylon University Press.
Nikāya Sangraha
Niti-Nighanduva
1880 Translated by C. J. R. Le Mesurier and T. B. Panabokke. Colombo: Government Printer.
NOWOTNY, Fausta.
1957 "Das Pūjāvidhinirūpaṇa des Trimalla".

Indo-Iranian Journal 1: 109–159.
OBEYESEKERE, Gananath
1963 "The Great Tradition and the Little in the Perspective of Sinhalese Buddhism". JAS 21: 139–154.
1966 "The Buddhist Pantheon in Ceylon and its Extensions". Anthropological Studies in Theravada Buddhism, M. Nash, ed., New Haven: Yale University Southeast Asia Studies: 1–26.
1967 Land Tenure in Village Ceylon: A Sociological and Historical Study. Cambridge: Cambridge University Press.
PARANAVITANA, S.
1928 "Mahayanism in Ceylon". The Ceylon Journal of Science, Section G, II, 1.
1929 "Religious Intercourse between Ceylon and Siam in the 13th–15 centuries". JCBRAS XXXII: 190–213.
1953 "The Shrine of Upulvan at Devundara". Archaeological Survey of Ceylon. Memoirs, Vol. VI: 19–59. Colombo: Government Printer.
1959 "Mahāyānism in Ceylon". Renè de Berval(ed). Présence du Bouddhisme, France-Asie XVI: 153–157, 515–527.
1960a "Lankatilaka Inscriptions". UCR 28: 1–45.
1960b "Ceylon and Malaysia in Mediaeval Times". JCBRAS VIII, 1: 1–42.
1966 Ceylon and Malaysia. Colombo: Lakehouse.
PERERA, Arthur A.
1920–1921 The Dayly Ritual at the Daladā Māligāva. CALR VI: 67–68.
PIERIS, Ralph
1956 Sinhalese Social Organization, the Kandyan Period. Colombo: The Ceylon University Press Board.
1967 "The Kandyan Kingdom, Political and Administrative Structure at the British Accession, 1815". Paper read at the XXVII Intern. Congress of Orientalists, Ann Arbor, Michigan.
PREMATILLEKE, L. and SILVA, R.
1968 "A Buddhist Monastery Type of Ancient Ceylon showing Mahāyānist Influence". Artibus Asiae XXX, I: 61–84.
POLATH-KEHELPANNALA, T. B.
1894 "New Year Ceremonies of the Kandyans". Monthly Literary Register II: 232–234, 246–247.
Pūjavaliya
1895 Translated by B. Guṇasēkera. Colombo: Ceylon Government Press.
RAGHAVAN, M. D.
1962 Ceylon, a Pictorial Survey of the Peoples and Arts. Colombo: M. D. Gunasena.
1964 India in Ceylonese History, Society and Culture. Bombay: Asia Publishing House.
RAHULA, Walpola
1956 History of Buddhism in Ceylon, the Anuradhapura Period 3rd Century BC—10th Century AC. Colombo: M. D. Gunasena.
RAJADON, Phya Anuman
1961 The Life of the Farmer. New Haven: HRAF Press.

Rājāvaliya
1900 Edited by B. Guṇasēkera. Colombo: Government Printer.
Ray, N.
1946 An Introduction to the Study of Theravada Buddhism in Burma. Calcutta: University of Calcutta.
Ray, M. C. *ed.*
1960 History of Ceylon, Vol. I, Part I From the Earliest times to 1505, Part II From the Cola Conquest in 1017 to the Arrival of the Portuguese in 1505. Colombo: Ceylon University Press.
Robinson, Marguerita S.
1965 The Role of Cooperative Labor in the Social Structure of a Sinhalese Village. Unpublished Ph. D. thesis, Harvard University.
1968a "The House of the Mighty Hero or the House of enough Paddy? Some Implications of a Sinhalese Myth", in: Dialectic in Practical Religion, E. R. Leach, ed. Cambridge: University Press: 122–152.
1968b "Some Observations on the Kandyan Sinhalese Kinship System". Man 3: 402–423.
Ryan, Bryce
1953 Caste in Modern Ceylon, a System in Transition. New Brunswick, N.Y.: Rutgers University Press.
Ryan, Bryce and Straus, Murray, A.
1954 "The Integration of Sinhalese Society". Research Studies of the State College of Washington, 22: 179–227.
Sarkisyanz, E.
1955 Russland und der Messianismus des Orients. Tübingen: Siebeck.
1965 Buddhist Backgrounds of the Burmese Revolution. The Hague: Martinus Nijhoff.
Sāsanāvatīrṇa varnanāva
n.d. Sinhalese ms., British Museum, Oriental Manuscripts Collection, Or. 6606(12) = Nevill Catalogue No. 20.
Sastri, K. A. Nilakanta
1958 A History of South India from Prehistoric Times to the Fall of Vijayanagar. London: Oxford University Press.
Seneviratne, H. L.
1961 "Some Aspects of the Negative Cult among the Sinhalese". CJHSS 4, 2: 149–151.
1963 "The Äsala Perahära in Kandy". CJHSS 6, 2: 169–180.
Seneviratna, John M.
1914 "Degraded Sinhalese Villages". JCBRAS XXIII: xxii–xxv.
Service tenure commission
1872 Service Tenure Register, Kandyan Provinces. Manuscript at the Kandy Kachcheri.
Sirr, Henry Charles
1850 Ceylon and the Cingalese. Vol. I, II. London: William Shoberl.
Smith, Donald E., ed.
1966 South Asian Politics and Religion. Princeton, N.J.: Princeton University Press.
SP = Sessional Paper. Colombo: Government Press.
Sessional Paper No. 1.

1956 Report of the Commission on Tenure of Lands of Viharagam, Dewalagam and Nindagam.
Colombo: Government Press.

SIEVERS, Angelika
1964 Ceylon, Gesellschaft und Lebensraum in den Orientalischen Tropen, eine sozialgeographische Landeskunde.
Wiesbaden: Franz Steiner Verlag.

SPIRO, Melford E.
1967 Burmese Supernaturalism. A Study in the Explanation and Reduction of Suffering.
Englewood Cliffs, N.J.: Prentice-Hall.

STOEHR, Waldemar and ZOETMULDER, Piet
1965 Die Religionen Indonesiens. Stuttgart: Kohlhammer.

STRAUS, Murray A.
1966 "Westernization, Insecurity, and Sinhalese Social Structure".
Intern. J. of Social Psychiatry 12: 130–138.

SWAY YOE
1882 The Burman, His Life and Notions. (reprinted 1958).

TAMBIAH, H. W.
1962 Buddhist Ecclesiastical Law.
JCBRAS 8, 1: 71–107.

TAMBIAH, S. J.
1958 "The Structure of Kinship and its Relationship to Land Possession and Residence in Pata Dumbara, Central Ceylon".
Journal of Royal Anthropological Institute 88: 21–44.
1965 "Kinship Fact and Fiction in Relation to the Kandyan Sinhalese".
JRAI 95, 2: 131–173.
1967 Review of Manning Nash et al., Anthropological Studies in Theravada Buddhism, New Haven: Yale University Southeast Asia Studies, 1966. Man 2, 1: 153.

TEMPLE LANDS COMMISSION
1856 Register of Temple Lands, Kandyan Provinces. Manuscript at the Kandy Katcheri.

VAḶPALA RĀHULA (Walpola Rahula)
1948 Bhikṣuvagē urumaya, Colombo, 2nd ed.

VIJAYAVARDHANA, D. C.
1953 Dharma-Vijaya (Triumph of Righteousness) or The Revolt in the Temple.
Colombo.

WALDSCHMIDT, Ernst.
1967 "Das Paritta, eine magische Zeremonie der buddhistischen Priester auf Ceylon".
in: Von Ceylon bis Turfan.
Göttingen: 456–478.

WALPOLA, Rahula *see* RAHULA, Walpola and VAḶPALA RĀHULA

WARNASURIYA, W. M. A.
1943 "Inscriptional Evidence bearing on the Nature of Religious Endowment in Ancient Ceylon".
University of Ceylon Review I, 1: 69–74; I, 2: 74–82.

WEBER, Max
1958 The Religion of India.
New York: The Free Press.

WHITE, Herbert.
1893 Manual of the Province of Uva.
Colombo: Government Printer.

WICKREMASINGHE, A. A.
1924 Land Tenure in the Kandyan Provinces.
Colombo: Maha Jana Press.

WINDISCH, E.

1895 Mara und Buddha.
Leipzig.

WIRZ, Paul.
1954a Exorcism and the Art of Healing in Ceylon.
Translated from the German (originally published in 1940).
Leiden: E. J. Brill.
1954b "Kataragama, die heiligste Stätte Ceylons". Verhandlungen der Naturforschenden Gesellschaft in Basel, Bd. 65, 2: 1–55.

WRIGGINS, W. Howard
1960 Ceylon, Dilemmas of a New Nation.
Princeton, N.J.: Princeton University Press.

YALMAN, Nur
1960 "The Flexibility of Caste Principles in a Kandyan Community", in Aspects of Caste in South India, Ceylon and North-West Pakistan, E. R. Leach, ed., Cambridge University Press.
Cambridge Papers in Social Anthropology No. 2: 78–112.
1962a "On some Binary Categories in Sinhalese Religious Thought".
Transactions of the New York Academy of Sciences, Ser. 2, 24.
1962b "The Ascetic Buddhist Monks of Ceylon".
Ethnology 1: 315–328.
1963 "On the Purity and Sexuality of Women in the Castes of Malabar and Ceylon".
JRAI 93: 25–58.
1964 "The Structure of Sinhalese Healing Rituals."
JAS, special issue, 23: 115–150.
1965 "Dual Organization in Central Ceylon or The Goddess on the Tree-top.
JAS 24: 441–457.
1967 Under the Bo Tree: Studies in Caste, Kinship and Marriage in the Interior of Ceylon.
London: Cambridge University Press and Berkeley and Los Angeles: University of California Press.

PLATE I

The "Great Royal Temple of Lankatilaka"

Plate II

The principal Buddha image in Lankatilaka Vihara

The Chief Monk of the vihāra (*vihārādhipati*) during flower offering

Plate IV

The Temple Lord of the devale (*basnāyaka nilamē*) during temple festival

The Buddhist monk during Buddha pujava (*tēvāva*)

PLATE VI

The Priest of the Gods (*Kapurāla*) during Deva pujava

Temple tenant plays the oboe during Buddha pujava

a. Temple tenants (*nilakāriya*) at the entrance to the temple of Dädimunda Devata Bandara

b. Procession during the New Rice Festival in Kandy